Propositions on
Christian Theology

Propositions on Christian Theology

A Pilgrim Walks the Plank

Kim Fabricius

CAROLINA ACADEMIC PRESS
Durham, North Carolina

Library of Congress Cataloging-in-Publication Data

Fabricius, Kim.
  Propositions on Christian theology : a pilgrim walks the plank /
by Kim Fabricius.
     p. cm.
  Includes bibliographical references.
  ISBN 978-1-59460-554-3 (alk. paper)
  1. Theology, Doctrinal. I. Title.

  BT75.3.F33 2008
  230--dc22

2008011662

Carolina Academic Press
700 Kent Street
Durham, North Carolina 27701
Telephone (919) 489-7486
Fax (919) 493-5668
www.cap-press.com

Printed in the United States of America

In memory of my father,
who would have been proud to see his prodigal in print —
but wouldn't have believed a word of it.

Contents

Foreword

Mike Higton

A foreword is meant to suggest, as pithily and incisively as possible, a possible route in to an otherwise forbidding book. But what is a foreword writer to do when the book to which he is welcoming readers is *nothing but* pith and incisiveness, *nothing but* a collection of inviting doors into its subject matter? This book does not need a foreword as much as it needs three hundred afterwords: it sets three hundred hares racing,[1] and invites the reader to chase each one of them as it runs on a track leading deep into the subject matter of theology.

Nevertheless, for all the lightness of touch, all the acidic puns, all the firework scatter of ideas, this is a serious book on serious business. Kim Fabricius is one of God's kidnappers, commissioned to take every thought captive to the triune God who comes to the world in Jesus Christ. His propositions are designed to captivate you, truss you up, and deliver you to the feet of the one whose grace upholds the world, who can crucify you and raise you up, who can cut the strings of delusion and despair by which your supposedly free life is bound — and to whom astonished worship and delighted service are the only proper response.

You will find some propositions in this book on dull sermons

---

1. 291.5 hares, to be precise. Or 281.5 if, like me, you prefer not to count the hares that Kim has persuaded to play baseball.

and others on holy laughter, some on the Nicene creed and others on the nature of heresy, some on human sexuality and others on all-too-human hypocrisy, some on the role of angels and others on the location of hell, and still others on fasting and feasting, peace and policing, grace and gratitude—but don't be fooled into thinking that it is simply a scattershot miscellany. Proposition by proposition, aphorism by aphorism, this book provides a solid training in how to *think* theologically—how to break and remake your thought in the light of God's grace.

Look, for instance, at the ten propositions on being human. You will find out that human being is contingent, self-contradictory, physical, spiritual, relational, responsible, ludic, doxological, Christ-like and glorified. You might read all this simply as a bricolage of good ideas, a commonplace book of clippings from years of theological reading. Or you might read it as some kind of catechism: a conceptual check-up, good for pointing out ways in which your own thinking about human nature needs repair or re-tuning—not providing the kind of systematic instructions you would need if you wanted to build a car from scratch, but the kind that can help you diagnose most of the typical rattles, lurches and collapses from which this make suffers. But (provided you take care to read the propositions on spirituality later in the book) you can also read these propositions as a manual of spiritual discipline: a mirror of self-examination (and so of church-examination and of world-examination), and a prompt to penitence, prayer, and praise. These are propositions that have the capacity, like all good theology, to get under your skin and to fester there. They are pithy and witty not so that you can race through and have done with them, but so that you can slow down and live with each one for a while. Think of each proposition as a hammer blow—and realise that you would do well to pause after each, just to check whether anything is broken.

Of course, you won't (and shouldn't) agree with all of them. Some of them will irritate you. Some of them will make you grind your teeth, That is just as it should be. But here's another good thing about the book. Broken down into propositions, mostly arranged in overs ten balls long, it is easy to keep score (though it will look more like a cricket than a baseball score). As you read it through, taking your time, working out where and why you agree and where and why you disagree, you can tot up exactly what percentage of it you agree with. And this in turn is great because— oh. Hold on a moment I was just about to say that this is great because it opens up whole new possibilities of a statistical approach to theological studies—but I've just remembered that there are a couple of propositions in the book about theology as a science, and I'm not sure that what I've just suggested lines up with what those propositions recommend. I hope you won't mind waiting here while I look those propositions up again, to check that I've not gone astray. I'll be back in a moment—unless, of course, another proposition distracts me on the way ...

No piracy, but there is a plank
to walk over seventy thousand fathoms,
as Kierkegaard would say, and far out
from the land. I have abandoned
my theories, the easier certainties
of belief. There are no handrails to grasp.

R. S. Thomas
from "Balance"[1]

---

1. R.S. Thomas, "Balance", in *Frequencies* (London: Macmillan, 1978).

Introduction

Insomnia can be a terrible affliction in church during the sermon; it's not much fun for the pastor in the manse either. But here is how a curse became a blessing.

One dreary morning in January 2006, just after midnight, sleepless in Swansea, South Wales, I was sitting at my desk, too agitated to read or surf or even watch TV. In desperation I turned to prayer. Not a chance. I was overwhelmed by distractions. But then I thought, "This might be a waste of time, but it is still prayer, isn't it?"

And then I had an idea: Why not put down some thoughts on prayer, particularly if they seem outrageous, or even idiotic. So I started typing, numbering my thoughts as I went along. At about seven or eight, I thought, "Hey, I've got a decalogue here!" So I rounded them off and polished them up, and then posted them on "Connexions", the blog of my colleague and good friend Richard Hall: "Ten Provocative Propositions on Prayer."

The feedback—the comments—astonished me. People liked them, found them stimulating and helpful. They were re-blogged, downloaded, and used for private reflection and group discussion. So a few weeks later, same insomnia, same purgatory, another idea: How about "Ten Propositions on Hell"? Done. Even more comments—but not all of them favorable! But that was fine, because though applause is great, my aim was to goad people into some lateral theological thinking by taking on a big theme in a punchy, conversational style (I'm from New York). My aim has never been to be systematic or comprehensive, but mischievously suggestive.

Next up was "The Trinity," which was posted not only on "Connexions" but also on "Faith and Theology," the brilliant blog of the young Australian theologian Dr. Benjamin Myers, where the positive response, often now from the academy, was overwhelming — and humbling. And from there, over the next eighteen months, I went on a roll, feeding Dr. Myers a steady supply of my "Propositions," and, immensely encouraged, watching and replying as they made their way around the blogosphere and out into churches and classrooms for worship and study.

Along the way the Propositions ceased to be propositions in the strict sense, as they expanded from terse theses into more substantial paragraphs, but the number stayed the same (with one-and-a-half exceptions) and the name stuck. I have further expanded many of them for publication, and revised them too, not least in response to the learned and astute comments they triggered. My work is now the work of others too, as, actually, it has always been. I don't think that I have had an original thought in my life. I'm an intellectual thief, though I try to acknowledge the sources of my goods when I fence them. Where I fail, please accept my apologies — and put it down to my memory, not my morals.

Linking some of my hymns with the propositions was an idea that came late in the day, but I like to think that on this occasion it was a case of catching the owl of Minerva just before take-off. Almost all the hymns pre-date the Propositions, which suggests that the hymns are the real texts of this little book, the Propositions commentary. You know the old saying *lex orandi, lex credendi* — it might well be re-phrased *lex canendi, lex credendi* (as any Methodist will tell you). Desmond Tutu says that you should never trust a bishop who can't dance. Likewise you should never trust a theologian who doesn't sing. In heaven doctrine is not done in prose: "The end is music."[1]

Finally, may I sing the praises of a few people: first, Dr. Myers, whose keen eye and judicious advice, while making me blush, have perhaps saved me from a more public embarrassment; and second, the folk at Carolina Academic Press, whose interest, attentiveness, and patience have been exceptional.

---

1. Robert Jenson, *Systematic Theology, Volume II* (New York: Oxford University Press, 1999), p. 369.

God in Christ

~

God is one, God is three

God is one, God is three,
not an "it", "he", or "she",
but a song, doh, ray, mi:
    God is in the singing,
    to the rhythm swinging:

> *Take a chance, chance, chance,*
> *join the dance, dance, dance,*
> *sing the song,*
> *swing along,*
> *to the mystic music.*

God is one, God is three,
the divine symphony,
love's the main melody:
    maestro of creation,
    orchestrates salvation:

God is one, God is three,
playing in harmony
music that sets us free:
    God is so surprising
    when he's improvising!

God is one, God is three,
infinite mystery,
touring in history:
    What a revelation!
    Give God an ovation!

Ten Propositions on the Trinity

1. The Trinity is not an optional doctrine, it is essential. God *is* Trinity. The Trinity is who God is. Robert Jenson goes so far as to claim that "Father, Son, and Holy Spirit" is God's name, the church's name for the God Israel calls Yahweh. Certainly the Trinity identifies God. Does the Trinity threaten God's unity? On the contrary, the Trinity inscribes and secures God's unity. God's unity is not *behind* God's threeness, God's unity is *in* God's threeness. This is not speculative mathematics, it is a descriptive theology of revelation.

2. The Trinity is not an academic doctrine thought up by clever scholars, rather it grew out of Christian experience, particularly the experience of worship; it expressed the early church's pattern of prayer *to* the Father, *through* the Son, *in* the Spirit. *Lex orandi, lex credendi*: the doctrine of the Trinity is liturgical exegesis. Moreover, the Trinity is a transformative, not a speculative doctrine. Its theological telos is personal conversion and virtuous living; it is a barren doctrine unless it issues in love.

3. The driving force of the development of the doctrine of the Trinity was Christological and soteriological: it served to articulate the Christian experience of salvation in Christ. The first Christians already knew God as Lord; through Jesus they came to know God as Jesus' Father, *Abba*, and Jesus as God's Son; while in the Spirit Jesus continued to be present to them, forming a family of prayer to the Father and building a community of witness to Christ.

4. The church's thinking was this: As God *discloses* himself in worship and salvation, so God must *be* in Godself. In the technical language of Karl Rahner's Rule: the "economic" Trinity is the "immanent" Trinity, and the "immanent" Trinity is the "economic" Trinity. God's eternity unfolds in God's time, in the history of Jesus of Nazareth, particularly as it climaxes in the

cross and resurrection, and will culminate in the parousia.
What you see is what you get, and what you get is what there
is, world without end, amen.

5. At the heart of the doctrine of the Trinity is God's *being-as-
communion* (John Zizioulas). God's unity is not monadic, it
is relational. The doctrine of the Trinity is the church's exegesis of I John 4:8b: "God is love." Father, Son, and Holy Spirit
mutually indwell each other in love, giving, receiving and returning love in an eternal dynamic of self-donation. The Greek
noun *perichoresis* (though philologically not derived from *chor-
eia*, "dance") is the technical term suggestive of this trinitarian "choreography," which is not, however, a circle dance but
personal participation, interpenetration, and exchange. It is
also a *danse macabre*: the ultimate and defining moment of
God's self-disclosure as triune is the cross of Christ.

6. If God is Trinity, do Jews — and Muslims — know nothing of
God? Not at all. God can be partly known without having been
fully identified. In fact, "the church's identification of the one
true God as the Trinity does not preclude, but rather requires,
that Abraham and his children know how to refer to this God,
and so are able to worship him".[1] Indeed the activity of the
Spirit in the world encourages the church to be open and at-
tentive to the presence of God not only in the major religions
but also amidst humanity and in creation as such.

7. Is the language of the Trinity sexist? Not at all. No responsible
theologian has ever thought of the Father and Son as male, nor
of the Spirit (as is currently fashionable) as female. The issue
is not *gender* but *personhood*. In fact, it is a strictly monothe-
istic God, not the Trinity, that is patriarchal — and oppressive.
Which is not to deny that trinitarian language has been ex-
ploited in sexist ways. It is, however, to warn against quack re-

---

1. Bruce Marshall, "Christ and the Cultures: The Jewish People and
Christian Theology", in Colin Gunton (ed.), *The Cambridge Companion to
Christian Doctrine* (Cambridge: Cambridge University Press, 1997), p. 97.

placement therapy—e.g. "Mother," or even "Creator," for "Father." Revelation constrains us not to put faith at the mercy of metaphor-makers with idealist ontologies that reduce being to function and threaten the divine identity.

8. Father, Son and Spirit are *constituted* by their mutuality: they are who they are *only* in their inter-relationships. So too human beings, made in the image of God: we are who we are only in relationship with others. Margaret Thatcher said that there is no such thing as society; on the contrary, there is no such thing as an individual: there are only persons-in-relationship. However we must not expect one-to-one correspondences between trinitarian and human (or ecclesial) relationships. To say that humanity is co-humanity is enough—and more than enough.

9. Clearly the Trinity is not an irrelevant doctrine, it has very practical—indeed political—implications. That God is essentially and eternally God-in-relationship of equality and mutual fellowship—could there be a more cogent critique of hierarchies of domination and exclusion, or of an economics of greed and exploitation? In an age where agency is reduced to will, and ethics turns on conflicts about power, the doctrine of the Trinity has truly revolutionary potential.

10. Finally, that God is Trinity means that God is *mystery*—a mystery not to be *explained*, but *entered*. God calls us to participate in his very being. As God's being in be-coming (Jüngel), the Trinity is open and ec-centric. To recalibrate Bonhoeffer's famous designation of Jesus, the Trinity is the God-for-others. In Rublev's beautiful icon of the Trinity, Father, Son, and Holy Spirit are seated around three sides of a (eucharistic) table. The fourth side awaits a guest. The Trinity is *hospitable*.

That we, too, may come to the picnic
With nothing to hide, join the dance
As it moves in perichoresis,
Turns about the abiding tree.
(W. H. Auden, "Compline," in *Horae Canonicae*)

Eternal Father, almighty Father

Eternal Father, almighty Father,
you made the heavens and formed the earth;
you shaped all creatures
with wondrous features,
and in time brought Jesus to birth.

Eternal Jesus, incarnate Jesus,
the one who sits at the Father's knee,
through human mother
became our brother,
lived and died for me, even me.

Eternal Spirit, life-giving Spirit,
love of the Father, love of the Son,
you live inside us
and safely guide us
through the church to worlds yet to come.

O Liberator, Son, and Creator,
we worship you, Lord, in song and prayer;
your soul is gracious,
your heart is spacious,
in your joyful being we share.

Ten Propositions on the Divine Perfections

1. In speaking of God's *perfections* rather than God's *attributes* I pay homage to Karl Barth's doctrine of God. When we speak of God we must speak in superlatives. Thus John Webster defines God's *holiness*, which is arguably the text of which the perfections are the exegesis, as God's "majestic incomparability." God, as Tina Turner might put it, is "simply the best."

2. And "better than all the rest"? Yes, there is no comparison: *Deus non est in genere.* Yet because God has revealed himself to us in Jesus of Nazareth, "the knowability of God" (Barth), we may speak of God in human language. Because through the Holy Spirit, the prayability of God, there is an *analogia fidei*, theological predication is possible. The Fourth Lateran Council's caveat against idolatry is correct—"Between the Creator and the creature no similitude can be expressed without implying a greater dissimilitude"; nevertheless verisimilitude there is. There is truthful speech about God, and it is the church's vocation to speak it, such that to remain silent, or to withdraw into apophaticism, would be strategies of disobedience, ingratitude, and indeed of idolatry itself. So too would any explication of the divine perfections that does not issue from the doctrine of the Trinity, which, in Christian theology, has a critical as well as a constructive function.

3. Two more points of prolegomena. First, the words we use to speak of God are not inadequate, nor are they only contingently related to God, rather (with Wittgenstein) they are *grammatically* related to God, they define what we *mean* by "God." D. Z. Phillips cites his mentor Rush Rees: "Winston Churchill may be Prime Minister and also a company director, but I might come to know him without knowing this. But I could not know God without knowing that he was the Father and Creator of all things. That would be like saying that I might come to know Churchill without knowing that he had a face, hands,

body, voice or any of the attributes of a human being."[1] "What Rees is saying," explains Phillips, "is that 'creator', 'grace' and 'love' stand to God, as 'face', 'hands', 'body', stand to 'human being'," they "are *synonyms* for God."[2] And the point could be expanded by saying that the God's perfections are not merely adjectival, they are both nouns and verbs: God does not merely have his perfections, he *is* and *does* his perfections.

4. Second, although the words we use to speak of the divine perfections are not inadequate, they become adequate only as their meaning is re-defined as God discloses himself to us in scripture. Obviously certain dictionary definitions, and not others, constitute a necessary point of departure in speaking of God — God is righteous, not deciduous! — but the nature of God's righteousness, as *sui generis*, cannot finally be determined by ordinary usage or extrapolation, but only by God's own interpolation. New wine bursts old skins. There is a semantic baptism in which our words are crucified and raised. The classic example is Luther's hermeneutical breakthrough precisely over the term *dikaiosyne theou* (the righteousness of God) in Romans 1:16–17, when the tormented Reformer came to see that the scholastic understanding of God's righteousness as "active" and punitive must give way to an evangelical understanding of God's righteousness as "passive" and saving.

5. We now turn, first, to three classical "metaphysical" divine perfections, which seem to me to be the three most misunderstood. First, God is *all-powerful*. Does God's omnipotence mean that he can do anything that is not logically contradictory? Does it make theological sense, for example, to say that God is more powerful than Satan? It does not. There are different *kinds* of power, and divine power and demonic power are

---

1. D. Z. Phillips, *The Problem of Evil and the Problem of God* (London: SCM Press, 2004), p. 189.

2. Ibid., p. 190.

incommensurable. Nor does it make sense to say that God has *chosen* divine over demonic power, as if God's will were primary and his nature secondary (the nominalist fallacy). On the contrary, God's nature is the grammar of God's will, which is a Wittgensteinian way of saying that God's being and acts are one. God is *love* (I John 4:8)—that is the defining divine perfection—and God is love from tip to toe. God's *only* power is the power of love, in which there is no domination, coercion, or violence. Such is the immanent perichoretic, self-giving, non-rivalrous love of the Trinity, economically embodied in the cross (and, as Luther said, *crux probat omnia*). "Omnipotence," writes T. F. Torrance, " ... is what God does, and it is from His 'does' rather than from a hypothetical 'can' that we are to understand the meaning of the term. What God does, we see in Christ."[3] Rowan Williams suggests that the mess we often get ourselves into here comes from the tendency to picture God as having a human psychology, only bigger. It is the same tendency that opens the Pandora's boxes both of Calvin's "horrible decree" of double predestination and of theodicists' pious pleadings.

6. Second, God is *all-knowing*. Does God's omniscience mean that God is a divine know-it-all? Does God know the future? If the answer is Yes, how do we avoid determinism or fatalism, and what happens to human freedom and prayer? If the answer is No, has God heard the joke about the open theist? I find this discussion a barren one. Maybe I'm just stupid. But maybe what we have here is a kind of theological antinomy, questions to which the answers are neither Yes nor No but, according to Robert Pirsig in *Zen and the Art of Motorcycle Maintenance*, "Mu," such that we have to "un-ask" the questions. Indeed a question like "Does God know all there is to know about motorcycle maintenance?" simply makes no theological

---

3. T. F. Torrance, cited in Alister E. McGrath, *T. F. Torrance: An Intellectual Biography* (Edinburgh: T&T Clark, 1999), p. 191.

sense. Perhaps we can begin to sketch a meaningful account of the divine omniscience by citing Cranmer's great Collect for Purity, which speaks of the God "to whom all hearts are open, all desires known, and from whom no secrets are hidden." Pannenberg refers to God's inescapability. I refer instead to the biblical concept of the divine *wisdom*, or, better, the *logos*, incarnate in Jesus, who knows us (John 6: 6), knows God (John 7:29), knows everything (John 21:17)

7. Third, God is *omnipresent*. The jaws of pantheism yawn. I will not enter! I rather like Daniel L. Migliore's take on the subject: "The truth of God's omnipresence is that God is *present everywhere* but *everywhere freely present*. God is present when and where and how God pleases. God is present to all creatures and in all events, but not in the same way."[4] What about the universe as the body of God (Sallie McFague)? The maw of panentheism opens. I will not enter it either! We may say that God is *in* the universe, and even that the universe is *in* God, but we must ensure that the former does not collapse into pantheism and the latter into panentheism. It is best to speak Christologically and pneumatologically. God is in Christ who descended to the depths, ascended to the heights, and fills the cosmos with his presence (Ephesians 4:7ff.). The wise God who is "acquainted with all my ways," whose "knowledge is too wonderful for me," is also the spacious God whom the Psalmist asks rhetorically, "Where can I go from your Spirit? Or where can I flee from your presence?" (Psalm 139: 3, 6, 7). But there is no cause for paranoia or claustrophobia: Robert Jenson delightfully speaks of "God's *roominess*."[5]

---

4. Daniel L. Migliore, *Faith Seeking Understanding: An Introduction to Christian Theology*, Second Edition (Grand Rapids, Michigan: William B. Eerdmans, 2004), p. 86.

5. Robert Jenson, *Systematic Theology, Volume I* (New York, Oxford University Press, 1997), p. 25.

8. Is God *impassible*? According to theologians like Moltmann and Jüngel, the cross has terminated the axiom of the divine *apatheia* and immutability. Yet this classical theological principle is not without value in its insistence that God's action is never reactive nor determined by anything other, rather God is "detached," not stoically but in the desert fathers' sense of detachment, which is not a psychological bolthole from the world, but the condition for spiritual engagement with the world free from fantasy and self-deception. Likewise God's *eternity* is not a disengagement from time. Rather "The true God is not eternal because he lacks time, but because he takes time";[6] indeed the very identity of his deity is defined by what God does in time—particularly around AD 30. God, in short, is not constrained, God is *free*, free even from the constraint of freedom, and therefore free to bind himself to humanity in Jesus Christ. Inside the doctrine of the divine impassibility is the doctrine of the divine freedom trying to get out.

9. And what of the divine *transcendence*? God's transcendence is God's Wholly Otherness (Barth). But just as infinity is *bad* infinity if it stands in contrast to finitude rather than taking finitude into itself (Hegel), so too God's transcendence is bad transcendence if it stands in contrast to God's immanence rather than taking immanence into itself. As Bonhoeffer wrote: "God's 'beyond' is not the beyond of our cognitive faculties. The transcendence of epistemological theory has nothing to do with the transcendence of God. God is beyond in the midst of our life."[7] Or as the later Barth himself came to understand, God is transcendent precisely as Immanuel, as God-with-us in the history of Jesus. This history is God's *mystery*.

---

6. Ibid., p. 217.
7. Dietrich Bonhoeffer, *Letters and Papers from Prison* (London: SCM Press, 1971 [first published in 1953]), p. 282.

10. Finally, if the *holiness* of God (with which we began) is the
    overture of the divine perfections, the *glory* of God is the sum
    of divine perfections (Barth). God is *beautiful*, radiantly beau-
    tiful. Again, however, Christologically re-defined, and there-
    fore counter-intuitive and counter-cultural: "he had no form
    or majesty that we should look at him, nothing in his appear-
    ance that we should desire him" (Isaiah 53:2). Indeed in John's
    gospel, the glory of Jesus is focused precisely on the cross:
    Christ is "drop-dead gorgeous." Nor is the resurrection a
    makeover but rather the revelation of the hidden glory of the
    crucified. But "the light of the knowledge of the glory of God
    in the face of Jesus Christ" (II Corinthians 4:6) — it is true that
    it is but the trailer of the feature to come at the eschaton, when
    indeed we ourselves "will be like him, for we will see him as
    he is" (I John 3:2), the "light of hyper-glory that the saints be-
    hold" (Gregory of Palamas). Ultimately, as we are drawn into
    the very triune life of God through the doxological work of the
    Holy Spirit (II Corinthian 3:18), we ourselves will share, pari
    passu, in the divine perfections.

Holy Spirit, sudden gust

Holy Spirit, sudden gust
   and darting tongue of flame,
one whose presence is a must
   or worship's limp and lame,
as we gather here to meet,
come and sweep us off our feet,
where we're cold, turn up the heat—
   it's new creation time!

Holy Spirit, gentle dove,
   all-animating breath,
you bear fruit in peace and love,
   you bring life out of death,
draw together those apart
with your reconciling art,
stimulate the stony heart—
   it's new creation time!

Holy Spirit, one of three,
   the God who goes between,
you declared the Jubilee
   through God the Nazarene,
through the church communicate
words and deeds that liberate,
and the world will be a fête—
   it's new creation time!

Ten Propositions on the Holy Spirit

1. Two's company, three's a crowd: pneumatology has always been the odd "ology" out in trinitarian thought. In the Nicene Creed (325), the third article is so minimalist it is almost a footnote. Only in the aftermath of Nicaea, mainly as a result of Basil of Caesarea duking it out with the Pneumatomachi, did the Holy Spirit get some extended creed cred at Constantinople in 381. Then there was the domestic bust-up between East and West over the *filioque* clause from the ninth century, leading to the messy divorce of 1054. In the twentieth century the Pentecostal and charismatic movements foregrounded the Spirit in the Western church, but, again, not without controversy. No doubt about it: while often rather anonymous, the Spirit is a holy troublemaker.

2. The Holy Spirit is God. By "appropriation," after a nod to creation, we tend to associate the Spirit with ecclesiology, and also with anthropology — the Spirit within us (as in Calvin's *testimonium internum*) and among us (as in John V. Taylor's "Go-Between"). And that's okay, indeed crucial — as long as there is no collapse into immanentism. But immanence is always ominously imminent: witness the pervasive influence of Kantian and Hegelian idealism, the historicism and subjectivism of liberal theology, and the ecclesiomonistic preoccupations of much postliberal theology. The Holy Spirit must never be confused with, collapsed into, or commandeered by the human spirit or the church. The Holy Spirit is God.

3. What about the *filioque*? Too much ink, let alone blood, has already been spilt on this contested issue for me to add to it. There are good biblical as well as patristic grounds for positions both pro and contra. The pneumatological advantages of a double procession include: a stress on the Spirit as personal being rather than impersonal force, a specific (Christological) content and criterion for discerning the spirits, a guard against lapsing into natural theology, pantheism, and fuzzy mysticism.

The pneumatological advantages of a single procession include: an assurance of the cosmic and global sweep of the Sprit's activity, a brake on Christomonism, a bulwark against dualism, modalism, and subordinationism. Of course the Western church, with its unilateral action, must take most of the blame for the Great Divorce. In my view, it should now retake the initiative, this time in reconciliation, with the widely accepted ecumenical formula that the Spirit proceeds "*from* the Father *through* the Son."

4. Is the Holy Spirit *feminine*? Don't be silly! *None* of the Trinitarian *personae* is gendered. And I'm afraid the Fathers would smile at any sisters (and brothers) who think they thought otherwise. Thus the idea that taking the Spirit to be feminine would provide a maternal balance to masculine and patriarchal Father-Son imagery rests on a mistake at source, quite misunderstanding the nature of trinitarian imagery and theological language. The intention of revisionists is to achieve a balanced differentiation, and thus transcendence, of the sexes in God, but I wonder if it doesn't rather just sex him/her up, misleading the church into a kind of Canaanite captivity. The Holy Spirit is neither he, she, nor it. The Holy Spirit is God.

5. And God is who God is in God's acts. What, then, does the Holy Spirit *do*? In the Old Testament, the Spirit is the divine dynamo that quickens life, empowers people, and inspires prophets. In the (synoptic) gospels, the Spirit quickens, empowers, and inspires Jesus. It is Luke, in particular, who highlights the intimate connection between the Holy Spirit and Jesus — in his birth, his baptism, his temptations, his Nazareth manifesto, his healings, his prayer-life, his passion — to which Paul adds his resurrection. "The Spirit," writes Kathryn Tanner, "radiates the humanity of Jesus."[1] Colin Gunton empha-

---

1. Kathryn Tanner, *Jesus, Humanity and the Trinity: A Brief Systematic Theology* (Edinburgh: T&T Clark, 2001), p. 53.

sizes the role of the Spirit as "the mediator of the Son's relation to the Father in both time and eternity," as the source of
the "otherness and particularity" of Jesus, and as the agent of
his freedom and obedience. Gunton also stresses that it is the
Spirit "who forms a body for the Son."[2]

6. Eugene F. Rogers picks up this theme in *After the Spirit: A Constructive Pneumatology from Resources outside the Modern West*
(2005), and extends the discussion to the resurrection and ascension—and to Pentecost and beyond. "The Spirit," he writes,
"characteristically befriends the body.... In the world, the Spirit
is not Person *or* thing, because the Spirit is Person *on* thing.
And the Spirit is Person on thing *because* the Spirit is Person
on Person. The Spirit rests on material bodies in the economy,
because she rests on the Son in the Trinity."[3] Following Rogers'
trajectory, I would suggest that there are rich pickings here for
a political pneumatology: the Spirit of Jubilee who inspires a
praxis of liberation and an economy of grace.

7. The church is itself a body-politic, instituted by the ascended
Christ, constituted as the *koinonia* of the Holy Spirit, the honest broker (if you like) of our communion with Christ and with
fellow Christians. Interestingly, however, *koinos* (unclean) is
the exact opposite of *hagios* (holy). And as Jesus crossed cultic boundaries, touching the unclean and declaring all foods
kosher, so we should think of holiness not as exclusion and
separation but as inclusion and participation. Which is to say
that it is not moral rectitude but the forgiveness of sins—*the
credal characteristic of the *communio sanctorum*—that dis-
tinguishes the citizenship and embodies the holiness of the

2. Colin Gunton, *Intellect and Action: Elucidations on Christian Theology
and the Life of Faith* (Edinburgh: T&T Clark, 2000), p. 80.

3. Eugene F. Rogers, *After the Spirit: A Constructive Pneumatology from
Resources outside the Modern West* (Grand Rapids, Michigan: William B.
Eerdmans, 2005), pp. 60, 62.

church. "There is no greater sinner than the Christian church," said Luther. Which is why in the ecclesial body-politic, the fifth petition of the Lord's Prayer and the practice of mutual confession are the center of the civics of sanctification.

8. The Holy Spirit gathers the church — in order to send the church. "The church exists by mission as fire exists by burning" (Emil Brunner). In his seminal *Transforming Mission*, David Bosch observes that whereas Paul relates pneumatology primarily to the church, "the intimate linking of pneumatology and mission is Luke's distinctive contribution to the early church's missionary paradigm.... For Luke, the concept of the Spirit sealed the kinship between God's universal will to save, the liberating ministry of Jesus, and the worldwide mission of the church."[4] Bosch also observes that while the early Fathers' pneumatology focused on sanctification and apostolicity, and the Reformers' on the role of Spirit in bearing witness to Word of God, it was only in the twentieth century that there was a rediscovery of the fundamentally missionary nature of the Holy Spirit.

9. Mission, however, transcends monological evangelism. Missionaries once commonly spoke of "the great unreached." Unreached by whom? Religious pluralism then? On the contrary, (a) I find the exclusivism-inclusivism-pluralism paradigm confused and unworkable, and (b) I resist a purely conversionist missiology precisely on the basis of a high Christology, a cosmic pneumatology, and a robust ecclesiology. "We know where the church is; it is not for us to judge where the church is not" (Paul Evdokimov). Thus the Holy Spirit inspires the church to engage in mission without closure, mission that does not predetermine the divine action, mission practiced as dialogue, a listening as well as a speaking witness. Indeed Rowan Williams

---

4. David Bosch, *Transforming Mission: Paradigm Shifts in Theology of Mission* (New York: Orbis Books, 1991), pp. 114–15.

warns of "the dangers of religious self-enclosure and claims to final legitimacy." He speaks of a "readiness for dispossession," and to break the logjam of the exclusivism-inclusivism-pluralism paradigm, points to a Christ who is "God's question, no more, no less. Being a Christian is being held to that question in such a way that the world of religious discourse may hear it."[5]

10. The Holy Spirit is the divine glorifer. After Moltmann, both Pannenberg and Robert Jenson find a direct connection between pneumatology and eschatology. Both accord an ontological priority to the future and link it to the Spirit: Pannenberg speaks of the future as God's mode of being, and Jenson of the Spirit as the future God is not only preparing but looking forward to. They both seem to bind God's deity to the perfecting work of the spirit, which is the apotheosis of creation. Although there are philosophical (Hegelian) problems with this vision, and theological dangers too, there is an awesome boldness, beauty, and grandeur to it. In the eschaton, the Holy Spirit is stage center, cover of anonymity blown, face-to-face in the faces of all the redeemed in their infinite variety. The end is doxology.

5. Rowan Williams, "The Finality of Christ", in *On Christian Theology* (Oxford: Blackwell, 2000), pp. 99, 104–105.

Imagine all the countless ways

Imagine all the countless ways
    that picture how the Savior saves.
We lift our hearts in thanks and praise
    for cruel cross and empty grave.

He draws together Greek and Jew,
    he razes walls and ends all strife;
not for a pre-selected few,
    but for the world he gives his life.

He pays the ransom, setting free
    the slaves of sin and selfishness;
he liberates us all to be
    the slaves of grace and righteousness.

He gives himself in sacrifice,
    unblemished lamb for sinners slain;
he gives himself, while men play dice,
    to expiate the crime of Cain.

He puts us right when we are wrong,
    as judge he takes the felon's place;
released disciples sing a song —
    the prosecution has no case.

Lord, finish now the world you planned —
    perfecting is the Spirit's art —
the world in Christ that you began,
    the world you love with all your heart.

Ten Propositions on Penal Substitution

1. The doctrine of penal substitution is a theory—or, better, a model—of the atonement, an extended metaphor that narrates how God reconciled the world to himself in Christ. It is one model, but it is not the only model. Indeed without radical recalibration, it is a theologically repugnant model with potentially vicious and disastrous social and political implications. For now, however, the point is this: while the early church dogmatically defined its Christology at the Council of Chalcedon (451), in its wisdom it left its soteriology underdetermined. Therefore penal substitution—or any other doctrine of the atonement—should not be deployed as a litmus test of faith. Stanley Hauerwas, with characteristic delicacy, says, "If you need a theory to worship Christ, worship your fucking theory!"

2. The doctrine of penal substitution finds its classical expression in the theology of John Calvin (1509–64), and its definitive form in the theology of Charles Hodge (1797–1878). Today it is the lynchpin of "sound" conservative evangelical theology. In essence it says that the divine justice demands that humanity must "pay the price of sin." We must be punished for our wickedness—and the sentence is death; but on the cross, Jesus identified himself with our sinful condition and died in our place, taking our sins to the grave with him.

3. It is usually claimed that the doctrine of penal substitution is Pauline (indeed, pre-Pauline), but Paul Fiddes observes that while Paul certainly thought of Christ's death in terms of "penal suffering" ("since Christ is identified with the human situation under the divine penalty"), Calvin's doctrine requires the additional idea of the "transfer of penalty"—and this "theory requires the addition of an Anselmian view of debt repayment and a Roman view of criminal law"[1] (Calvin, remember, was trained

---

1. Paul Fiddes, *Past Event and Present Salvation: The Christian Idea of Atonement* (London: Darton, Longman and Todd, 1989), p. 98.

as a lawyer). A fortiori, to cite patristic evidence for the doctrine is anachronistic.

4. It is also usually claimed that St. Anselm (c. 1033–1100) anticipated Calvin. Insofar as Calvin was dependent on Anselm's view of debt repayment, and also added to Anselm's feudal emphasis on the compensation of God's *honor* his own late medieval emphasis on the expiation/propitiation of God's *wrath*, this claim is true. However, for Anselm, unlike Calvin, punishment and satisfaction are not equivalents but alternatives — *aut poena aut satisfactio*. That is, for Anselm Christ is not punished in our place, rather he makes satisfaction on our behalf. Therefore Anselm does not propound a doctrine of penal substitution. "Indeed, in the end," according to David Bentley Hart, "Anselm merely restates the oldest patristic model of atonement of all: recapitulation."[2]

5. If the doctrine of penal substitution is to have any place in contemporary soteriology, there are certain elements of its demotic form that have to be eliminated: namely, the notion that Jesus died to placate or appease God, or to secure a change in God's attitude, or to settle a score or balance the books — or, indeed, the notion that the cross is itself a divine punishment. Rather than drive such a wedge a between God and Jesus, the cross expresses their unity and mutual love. It is not a matter of anger or honor but of rescue and risk, obedience and self-sacrifice, of putting the world (Anselm's *ordo universi*) to rights and making it beautiful again. Penal substitution is often narrowly construed in individualistic and moralistic terms, so that the *cosmic* and *re-creational* scope of the atonement is marginalized or missed altogether.

6. God does not will the death of Jesus *tout court*, nor punish Jesus for our sins. The "necessity" of the cross cannot be con-

---

2. David Bentley Hart, *The Beauty of the Infinite* (Grand Rapids, Michigan: William B. Eerdmans, 2003), p. 371.

figured in these terms. Herbert McCabe: "The mission of Jesus from the Father is not the mission to be crucified; what the Father wished is that Jesus should be human.... [T]he fact that to be human means to be crucified is not something that the Father has directly planned but what we have arranged."[3] That is, the crucifixion is not a penalty inflicted by God but what inescapably, inevitably happens when human sin encounters divine love. The cross, therefore, represents the wrath and judgement of God not *directly* but *indirectly*: God "gives us up" (*paredoken*) (Romans 1:24, 26, 28) to the consequences of our destructive desires and deeds, the human condition with which Christ identified himself in life, and to which God "gave him up" (*paredoken*) (Romans 8:32), and to which we (with Judas) "betrayed"/"handed him over" (*paredoken*) (e.g. Mark 3:19), in death.

7. Expounders of the doctrine of penal substitution often elide the juridical with the sacrificial. This is a mistake: the law court, not the temple, is the metaphorical setting of this model. Sacrifice, in the Bible, is never punitive; rather, it is a divine gift, which, as human offering, becomes an expression of praise and gratitude. It is also a demonstration that reconciliation is a costly matter. But justice too, in the Bible, is not essentially punitive or retributive, it is restorative. If we continue to think of the atonement in forensic terms, it is essential to see it not as a legal transaction but as the *transformation of a relationship*. No cross without a resurrection — and no justification without sanctification — connections not always convincingly made by advocates of the doctrine of penal substitution.

8. Substitution — or representation? Did Jesus die "in our place" or "on our behalf"? The debate is barren: both are true. They are, as Colin Gunton says, "correlative, not opposed concepts.

---

3. Herbert McCabe, *God Matters* (London: Continuum, 1987, 2005), p. 93.

Because Jesus is our substitute, it is also right to call him our representative."[4] But, again, it is in the court, not the cult, that substitution gets its metaphorical purchase: in Christ the judge steps into the dock and is judged in our place (Karl Barth). And, again, the theme is God's liberating initiative, not the demands of the law. "The centre of the doctrine of the atonement is that Christ is not only our substitute—'instead of'—but that by the substitution he frees us to be ourselves. Substitution is *grace*"[5]—and grace, not sin, runs the show.

9. Nevertheless, others—particularly students of René Girard—declare that penal substitution is an inherently *violent* model of the atonement; moreover, that it underwrites a culture of brutality and vengeance, ethically, socially, and politically. Radical feminist theologians Joan Carlson Brown and Rebecca Parker have gone so far as to speak of "divine child abuse," and argue that the model's image of Jesus voluntarily submitting to innocent suffering contributes to the victimization of women. Black liberation theologian James Cone links the model to defenses of slavery and colonialism. Michael Northcott suggests that it is no coincidence that leaders of the Religious Right, for whom the model is so central, are such staunch advocates of the *lex talionis*, capital punishment, and the war on terror. Yet even Miroslav Volf, hardly a conservative evangelical, argues that "the only way in which non-violence and forgiveness will be possible in a world of violence is through *displacement* or *transference* of violence, not through its complete relinquishment."[6]

4. Colin Gunton, *The Actuality of Atonement* (Edinburgh: T&T Clark, 1988), p. 166.

5. Ibid.

6. Miroslav Volf, *Exclusion and Embrace: A Theological Exploration of Identity, Otherness, and Reconciliation* (Nashville: Abingdon Press, 1996), p. 302.

10. I am unconvinced and find myself finally opposed to the idea of divine violence. While the deity of penal substitution may not be the Aztec god Huitzilopochtli (the one with the taste for hearts), he certainly does not look like the God Jesus called *Abba*. I do not see how divine violence can be squared with *this* God. How can I say such a thing? The doctrine of the Trinity! If *opera trinitatis ad extra sunt indivisa*, and if the economic Trinity reveals the immanent Trinity, how can the Spirit-anointed Jesus of Nazareth, who rejected the *lex talionis*, have a vengeful Father? How can an economy of exchange issue from an economy of extravagance? Not surprisingly, expositors of the doctrine of penal substitution usually isolate the cross not only from the resurrection of Jesus, but also from his life and teaching; but if you talk about the death of Christ apart from the life and teaching of Christ then you are not talking about the death of *Christ*. To rephrase I John 1:5: "This is the message we have heard from him and proclaim to you, that God is non-violent, and in him is no violence at all." The work of Barth, Moltmann, and Jüngel is an indispensable resource for thinking through the implications of the inextricable relationship between the doctrine of the Trinity and a *theologia crucis*. A doctrine of substitution is still serviceable, indeed it is essential, but understood not in *penal* but in *ontological* terms: that Christ dies "in our place" (as our substitute) — and "on our behalf" (as our representative) — is a soteriological expression of our "being in Christ," of our participation in the life of the triune God.

Lord Jesus Christ, your mighty resurrection

Lord Jesus Christ, your mighty resurrection
  fills us with overwhelming joy and fear,
as you begin your world-wide insurrection,
  and lead the way as faith's great pioneer.

Your cross proclaims the depths of our corruption,
  your empty tomb the heights of grace sublime,
your risen power causes an eruption
  of love exploding out through space and time.

You lived a life of challenge, trust, and service,
  you suffered death in doubt and agony,
you live again and stride ahead with purpose,
  and bring your friends along for company.

As risen Lord, you call us all to mission,
  embracing people, creatures, earth, and stars,
you give to each a personal commission
  to share your healing as we bear your scars.

Exalted Christ, the victim's vindication,
  we follow in the slipstream you release,
propelled by promise of the new creation
  when the whole universe will be at peace.

Ten Propositions on the Resurrection

1. Can there be any day but this,
   Though many sunnes to shine endeavour?
   We count three hundred, but we misse:
   There is but one, and that one ever.
   —George Herbert, "Easter"

   The resurrection in propositions? May the poets forgive me!

2. The most prosaic of approaches to the resurrection are those
   apologetics modeled on courtroom drama: the authors invite the
   gospel witnesses to take the stand, elicit their testimonies, cross-
   examine them, explain away any inconsistencies or contradictions, dismiss the counter-evidence—and the defense rests:
   that Christ is risen is beyond reasonable doubt. But Rowan
   Williams objects—and the objection is sustained: "As far as the
   historical question goes, it is clear that the scholarly analysis of
   the resurrection narratives has not yielded a single compelling
   resolution to the numerous difficulties that the texts pose."[1]

3. And (to switch metaphors from the courtroom to the operat-
   ing theater) were the operation successful, the patient would be
   dead on the table. How so? Because the resurrection is "a para-
   phrase of the word 'God'" (Karl Barth)—and God is ultimate
   mystery. God is no *deus ex machina* who, in raising Jesus from
   the dead, provides dramatic closure, or, for that matter, secures a happy ending.

   It was by negatives I learnt my place.
   The garden went on growing and I sensed
   A sudden breeze that blew across my face.
   Despair returned but now it danced, it danced.
   —Elizabeth Jennings, "The Resurrection"

---

1. Rowan Williams, "Between the Cherubim: The Empty Tomb and the
Empty Throne", in *On Christian Theology* (Oxford: Blackwell, 2000), p.183.

4. Am I saying that the resurrection was not an historical event? That depends. If your understanding of "historical" is based on the famous criteria of Ernst Troeltsch — probability, relativity, and analogy — then, no, it was not an historical event. But why, asks Wolfhart Pannenberg, accept these criteria? Why accept a definition of history that rules out, *ab initio*, the singular and unique (and its presupposition of an ontology incarcerated in immanence)? Yet Pannenberg also maintains that the conventions of modern historiography, including its procedures of proof, can successfully be applied to the appearances of the risen Jesus, such that we can infer the resurrection from the evidence. And that is where I part company with Pannenberg and join Barth: the resurrection is an impossible possibility. It is historical — it happened in space and time — but it is not historically demonstrable. It is, in principle, historically falsifiable, but not historically verifiable. The resurrection rends and ruptures the causal nexus of history; indeed, as the crucifixion is the apocalyptic end of the world, the resurrection is *creatio ex nihilo* (cf. Romans 4:17). With Moltmann, its verification can only be eschatologically ascertained in the new heaven and the new earth. Between the times, the "proof" of the resurrection is — the church!

5. "The point of the appearances is precisely the arising of faith in the Risen One. He did not show himself to everyone, he did not become an object of neutral observation. Nor can one say that the appearances presupposed faith in him. Rather, those to whom they occurred became believers." True, "in every case knowledge of Jesus is presupposed, and that means that the question of faith has already been raised.... But the witness of faith is recognised only when one accepts his witness in faith."[2]

6. Was the tomb empty? Of course! Not least because in first-century Judaism it would have been semantically impossible for

---

2. Gerhard Ebeling, *The Nature of Faith* (London: Collins, 1961), pp. 68–69.

the word "resurrection" to describe an afterlife in which the physical body was left to the grave. The (liberal) notion of a "spiritual" resurrection is irredeemably docetic. It is the perishable, corruptible physical body that must put on immortality (I Corinthians 15:53). Nor should we miss the gnostic understanding of creation—and the new creation—that is implicit in a Jesus who is risen only in our hearts—or, for that matter, in the kerygma (Bultmann). "Let us not mock God with metaphor" (writes John Updike):

Make no mistake: if He rose at all
it was as His body;
if the cells' dissolution did not reverse, the molecules
    reknit, the amino acids rekindle,
the Church will fall.
—John Updike, "Seven Stanzas at Easter"

7. I sense the same docetism in those who would elide the resurrection with the cross. It is quite true that the resurrection is not the reversal of a defeat but the proclamation of a victory, not the abrogation of the cross but its inner meaning. So Eberhard Jüngel is quite right to say that the resurrection does not cancel the cross but establishes it. But he is quite wrong to conclude that the resurrection is not a discrete event subsequent to the crucifixion. Hans Urs von Balthasar's theology of Holy Saturday stands as a warning to such a collapse of Easter Sunday into Good Friday. And so too does I. H. Marshall's recent insistence on the importance of the resurrection, as well as the cross, in a truly biblical theology of the atonement.

8. It is characteristic for the risen Christ to greet his disciples with the word *Shalom*: "Peace be with you!" He calms their fear—of retribution, perhaps? After all, these were the men who, despite their protestations of loyalty, had abandoned their master to his fate. Perhaps now it was payback time for their betrayal? And what of Caiaphas and Pilate and all who had connived in the murder of Jesus—might we not expect a risen Terminator: "I'll be back—and this time it's personal"? Chris-

tian pacifists are often accused of arguing their case from the Crucified who refuses the way of violence. But the power of pacifism equally comes from the Risen One who refuses the way of vengeance. The Judge is the condemned Victim. How can he not be merciful?

So let us love, deare Love, like as we ought,
— Love is the lesson which the Lord us taught.
— Edmund Spenser, "Easter Sunday"

9. The risen Christ meets no one without calling them to witness and service. The meaning is in the mission. In fact, the resurrection of Jesus leads to two missions. Did you ever notice that, according to Matthew (28:11), it is the soldiers, professional killers, who first bring news of the events at the tomb to Jerusalem — to the chief priests, who then bribe them and commission them to spread a lie about what had happened (28:12–15)? By contrast, in the closing verses (28:16–20), Jesus commissions the disciples to make more disciples, teaching them what they had learned from Jesus (fundamentally, the Sermon on the Mount). Lies and violence, very lucrative — that is the one mission. Truth and peace, very costly — that is the other mission. On this mission, the risen Christ said, "I am with you always, to the end of the age."

10. Finally eschatology (of course!) — or doxology. "Jesus," says Robert Jenson, "is risen into the future that God has for his creatures. What certain persons saw after his death was a reality of that future."[3] Which is another way of saying that Jesus is risen into the glory of God. The resurrection is, as it were, the coming attractions of the Coming Attraction, the human being fully alive who is the glory of God (Irenaeus).

---

3. Robert Jenson, *Systematic Theology, Volume I* (New York: Oxford University Press, 1997), p. 198.

In a flash, at a trumpet crash,
I am all at once what Christ is, since he was what I am, and
This Jack, joke, poor potsherd, patch, matchwood,
    immortal diamond,
                        Is immortal diamond.
—Gerard Manley Hopkins,
"That Nature Is a Heraclitean Fire and of the Comfort of the
Resurrection"

Children die from drought and earthquake

Children die from drought and earthquake,
   children die by hand of man.
What on earth, and what for God's sake,
   can be made of such a plan?
Nothing—no such plan's been plotted;
   nothing—no such plan exists:
if such suffering were allotted,
   God would be an atheist.

Into ovens men drive "others",
   into buildings men fly planes;
history's losers are the mothers,
   history's winners are the Cains.
Asking where was God in Auschwitz,
   or among the Taliban:
God himself was on the gibbets—
   thus the question: Where was man?

God of love and God of power—
   attributes in Christ are squared.
Faith can face the final hour,
   doubt and anger can be aired.
Answers aren't in explanation,
   answers come at quite a cost:
only wonder at creation,
   and the practice of the cross.

Ten Propositions on Theodicy

1. *Unde malum* (Whence evil)? Primers on theodicy easily put
    the question: God is supposed to be both all-loving and all-
    powerful, yet evil and suffering demonstrably exist. Therefore
    either God *can* do something about it but *won't*—in which
    case God is not all-loving; or God *wants* to do something about
    it but *can't*—in which case God is not all-powerful. Gotcha!
    Or so it would seem.

2. It is quite astonishing that Christians have allowed themselves
    to be set up in this way—or at least post-Enlightenment Chris-
    tians. For as Kenneth Surin points out, "It is no exaggeration
    to say that virtually every contemporary discussion of the theod-
    icy question is premised, implicitly or explicitly, on an under-
    standing of 'God' overwhelmingly constrained by the principles
    of seventeenth and eighteenth century philosophical theism."
    And Surin goes on to observe that the 'God' this discussion
    seeks "to justify is the very 'thing' that the adherent of a prop-
    erly Christian 'understanding' of God will find herself being
    disposed to abjure."[1] Of course pre-modern Christians wrestled
    with the reality of evil and suffering, but their faith was not
    intimidated by it, nor did it throw their belief in the divine
    goodness into a crisis of coherence. *Unde malum*? Rather *Quis
    Deus* (Who is God)? Not the god of theism (onto-theology)
    who is discussed *remoto Christo*, but God the Trinity, who is
    known in worship.

3. Alas, many Christian theologians themselves do not seem to
    know this God. They think God requires an apologetics, and
    their defense takes the form of accusation and explanation.
    First, they are Job's comforters, resembling "a circle of police
    around a suspect" (René Girard), reading a list of the charges

---

1. Kenneth Surin, *Theology and the Problem of Evil* (Oxford: Basil
Blackwell, 1986), pp. 4, 7.

to the suspect from Uz; and then they are attorneys for God in the dock, arguing the case of their client *in absentia* with cool calculation and untroubled conviction. The irony is that in explaining evil and suffering, theodicists inevitably explain them away. Wittgenstein said that "what's ragged should be left ragged," but the post-Cartesian theodicist, intent on systematic closure, not only sweetens the bitterness of evil but also, in his theoretical detachment, connives in the conditions that give them purchase; and in making a pact with death in order to defend the deity, he unwittingly turns God himself into a capital criminal.

4. Theologians following philosophers like John Hick and Richard Swinburne are the great *explainers*. Their strategy turns on free will. Evil, they urge, is the inevitable risk of moral human being, and if it results in sin and its attendant wreckage, well, (a) we can't blame God; and (b) still, this valley of death is also a vale of soul-making (i.e. suffering has pedagogical or therapeutic value). The decisive criticism against this "free-will defense" is its competitive understanding of divine and human agency, as if freedom were a zero-sum game — we can only have more if God has less — which in fact is idolatrous because it reduces God to the status of a creature. But there is also the question: How real is our freedom? And further: Can our bad choices alone account for the sheer scale of suffering? And again: Can so-called second-order virtues bear the burden of vindication that is placed upon them? Or does not the buck stop on the divine desk? Marilyn McCord Adams declares that, given "horrendous evils" — the physical agony and the eclipse of meaning (what Simone Weil called "affliction") — this putative god would be paying us "an inappropriate respect," and indeed "would not thereby *honor* but *violate* our agency by crushing it with responsibility for individual and cosmic ruin."[2]

---

2. Marilyn McCord Adams, *Horrendous Evils and the Goodness of God* (Ithaca: Cornell University Press, 1999), p.48.

And D. Z. Phillips refers to the argument from character development as "the outward-bound school of theology," and
suggests that "to rescue sufferings from degradation by em-
ploying cost-benefit analysis is like rescuing a prostitute from
degradation by telling her to charge higher fees."[3] Holocaust
survivors themselves tells us that concentration camps are not
ideal places for inculcating virtues in those who experience or
witness extreme suffering.

5. Calvinists are the great *defenders.* David Bentley Hart writes
   of a Calvinist minister who, "positively intoxicated by the
   grandeur of divine sovereignty, proclaimed that the Indian
   Ocean disaster — like everything else — was a direct expression
   of the divine will, acting according to hidden and eternal counsels it would be impious to attempt to penetrate, and produc-
   ing consequences it would be sinful to presume to judge."[4] More
   extreme still are the false prophets who thundered that the
   denizens of the Sodom of New Orleans only got what was coming to them when the whirlwind of Katrina tore into the city.
   I admit to finding this whole track of retributive thought so
   unbearably desolate that I will only say, in answer, that here
   we see the dead and deathly end of late medieval nominalism,
   see that *potentia absoluta* is at best a theological solecism, and
   at worst sheer satanic power. It is also the inevitable result of
   the deity known in abstraction from the concrete reality of
   Christ. God *cannot* will evil and suffering, either directly or
   indirectly.

6. And here we come to the nub of the matter. The divine nature
   is the grammar of the divine will. God's actions are identical
   with God's being; who God is and what God does are one. And
   in being and act, God is love — all the way down and all the

3. D. Z. Phillips, *The Problem of Evil and the Problem of God* (London:
SCM Press, 2004), pp. 66, 71.

4. David Bentley Hart, *The Doors of the Sea: Where Was God in the
Tsunami?* (Grand Rapids: William B. Eerdmans, 2005), p. 27.

way out. The conundrum of the divine love and the divine
power that theodicists accept and then attempt to resolve is
thus a false one. God is not all-loving on the one hand and all-
powerful on the other: no, the *only* power of God is the power
of love.

Here is God, no monarch he,
throned in easy state to reign;
here is God, whose arms of love
aching, spent, the world sustain.
(W. H. Vanstone)

7. Rejecting, then, the Calvinist collapse of secondary into primary divine causality, shall we say that God *permits* the evil
that is contrary to his will? Philosophically (with Aquinas) it would
seem to be a necessary distinction to make, but I remain uncomfortable with the language of permission, and for two reasons. First, I am uncomfortable because it suggests that God
is a moral agent with a psychology just like ours only bigger, con-
juring up a fatuous image of one who has to make allowances
for the world to be other than he really intends it to be, as if—
give the deity a break—God was doing the best he could. Here
lies the fundamental fallacy of process theodicies. And second,
I am uncomfortable because we are still playing the game of
explanation. Evil, we must insist, cannot and must not be explained. If the language of permission still seems inescapable,
then, continuing to insist that the free-will defense is a busted
flush, we must confess that we don't have the faintest idea *why*
God permits evil. The language of permission is permissible
only as an expression of the agonising distance between the
"already" of the resurrection and the "not-yet" of the parousia. Ultimately we can only gaze at the iconic image of the crucified Christ and, like a rabbit caught in a car's headlights,
freeze at the mystery of human iniquity—and then, in faith,
be drawn into the more unfathomable mystery of divine love.

8. We must also be modest with the discourse of eschatology. Certainly we must hold fast to the vision of "a new heaven and a

new earth," when God "will wipe away every tear from their eyes. Death will be no more; mourning and crying and pain will be no more, for the first things have passed away" (Revelation 21:1, 4). But two points. First, *hell*. Whatever the Bible says to the contrary—and the Bible actually says many things to the contrary of the contrary—it beats me how an eternal Auschwitz (under a righteous commandant to be sure) could provide an adequate retributive balance to the temporal Auschwitz. If for some the idea of hell performs a successful operation in the theatre of theodicy, for me it kills the patient. And second, *children*. When we speak of the glory of the ultimate, we must not out-shout the cries of the penultimate; we must speak softly and tenderly, and never say anything that we could not say, paradigmatically, in the presence of parents who have watched their child torn limb from limb by a pack of hunting dogs, or tossed to and fro on soldiers' bayonets.

9. The images, of course, come from Dostoevsky's unsurpassable *The Brothers Karamazov*, as Ivan challenges the faith of his little brother, a novice monk, with a rending litany of human depravity, and then declares that "It is not God that I do not accept, Alyosha. I merely most respectfully return him the ticket," i.e. to the slaughter-house of history. Mark well that Ivan is not an atheist, he is a rebel. He has been to the house of God and knows its liturgies better than many a believer—but he cannot kneel and he will not pray. And also mark well that Alyosha accepts Ivan's argument that human freedom, ultimate victory, everlasting punishment, all finally fail to persuade: he refuses to offer a defense that would make God morally repugnant, and thus concedes the case that the universe is not morally intelligible. Theoretically, nihilism triumphs ...

10. ... But, practically, nihilism fails. It can be thought, but not lived: Ivan himself becomes a monster, twisting the mind of his half-brother Smerdyakov, turning him into a patricide—and he himself finally commits suicide. But Father Zosima presents Alyosha with an alternative—not an alternative *explanation* but an alternative *praxis*, presupposing conversion and issuing

in compassion for the afflicted, non-violent resistance against wickedness, and agnostic acceptance disturbed by restless lament, protest, and hope (of which George Steiner says "there is no word less deconstructible"[5]), all mediated by the church, the harbinger of horror-healing. It is participation in God's own triune love overflowing in the cosmos, and in the universal salvation wrought by the atoning death of Christ. The logical problem of evil and suffering is not thereby solved, rather it is dissolved in the existential narrative of discipleship. As my hymn concludes:

Answers aren't in explanation,
answers come at quite a cost:
only wonder at creation,
and the practice of the cross.

---

5. George Steiner, *Real Presences* (Chicago: University of Chicago Press, 1991), p. 232.

Christ in Us

God of all ages, ageless Lord

God of all ages, ageless Lord,
whose thoughts are deep, whose love is broad,
we of all ages offer praise
throughout the length of all our days.

We praise you for our wondrous birth,
formed from your breath and blessed earth,
shaped in the womb by your own hand—
miracle!—who can understand?

We praise you for the years of youth,
time to explore the realms of truth,
stretching our muscles and our minds,
testing new models of mankind.

We praise you for our grown-up years,
with their demands, their joys and fears;
taking the world you give in trust,
working to make it fair and just.

We praise you for retiring age,
as we approach life's final page;
still things to do, still sights to see,
but, most of all, we learn to be.

This is our life, from birth to death,
from infant's cry to final breath;
this is our life, our gift to you,
who gave it first, who'll make it new.

Ten Propositions on Being Human

1. To be human is to be *contingent*. This has to be said first because while ontologically it is rather obvious, existentially it is deeply problematical. One way or another, we all *know* that we are not necessary, that we are here without a by-your-leave, that we have been pitched into existence—whether by a vicious fastball, a deceptive slider, or a graceful curve depends on your faith—or, better, your *trust*. But human beings do not *live* this knowledge of contingency. Gifts of God to the world, we live like we are God's gift to the world. Elected, created, and called, we act like we are self-selected, self-made, self-choosing, necessary, as though our non-existence were inconceivable. We act, in other words, like God. And in acting *like* God we act *against* God. We sin.

2. To be human is to be *self-contradictory*. Sin is a surd, or, as Barth said, an impossible possibility. That is why we cannot fit sin into any system: it is inherently inexplicable, irrational—it doesn't compute. To be human is also to be self-contradictory in the sense that in acting against God, we act against ourselves: we are self-destructive—we are always hitting our delete key. Indeed, left to ourselves we would destroy ourselves, irretrievably, which is not only murder but also intended mass murder, for in destroying ourselves we would destroy the world. Homicide is always misdirected suicide. War always begins with a blitzkrieg on the self. Augustine's *amor sui*, self-love, is, in fact, self-hatred.

3. To be human is to be *physical*. We are made from earth, we return to the elements, but the human form is a wonder to behold: "the head Sublime, the heart Pathos, the genitals Beauty, the hands and feet Proportion" (Blake). And Ambrose, the fourth century bishop of Milan, said that "the movement of the body is an index of the soul." God has a body, but theologians like Sallie McFague are wrong when they suggest that the world is God's body. God has his own body—the body of

Christ. God is Spirit, but to think about God you have to think body, because the Word became flesh. Further, to be human is to be *sexual*. Desmond Tutu once said that Adam's first word upon awakening from the surgery that issued in Eve was "Wow!" To which Eve no doubt replied, "You're not so bad yourself!"

4. To be human is to be *spiritual*. But not, needless to say, spiritual as *against* somatic (or sexual!). Unlike Greek anthropology, Christian anthropology is not dualist, it understands human beings as ensouled bodies/embodied souls. Faith itself, Luther said, "is under the left nipple." Hence the crypto-gnosticism of any *soma sema* (the body is a tomb) "withdrawal" spirituality. The disembodied Cartesian ego would be a solipsistic hell were it not, in fact, a fiction. Thought itself is not a secret, hermetic activity. We may speak of the "inner life," of "interiority," writes Rowan Williams, but it "is neither a flight from relation, nor the quest for an impossible transparency or immediacy in relation, but that which equips us for knowing and being known *humanly*, taking time with the human world".[1]

5. To be human is to be *relational*. Again, of course: because God, as Trinity, is relational. God's being-as-communion is reflected in humans being-in-community. Jesus was the "man for others" (Bonhoeffer). Humanity is co-humanity: our being is "exocentric" (Pannenberg). Margaret Thatcher notoriously said that there is no such thing as society; on the contrary, there is no such thing as autonomy. Here lies the bankruptcy of all social contract theory. Further, as relational, social beings, we are *linguistic* beings, modelled on the *Deus loquens*. Here lies the theological import of Wittgenstein's observation that there is no such thing as a private language. Finally, to be relational means to be *dynamic*: our being is in our becoming. Here lies the inadequacy of Boethius' definition of a "person" as "an in-

---

1. Rowan Williams, "The Suspicion of Suspicion: Wittgenstein and Bonhoeffer", in Richard H. Bell (ed.), *The Grammar of the Heart* (San Francisco: Harper & Row, 1988), pp. 50–51.

dividual substance": it suggests not only isolation instead of sociality but also a subject without a predicate. The human is a happening. We are gerunds.

6. To be human is to be *responsible*. That is the inner meaning of the "dominion" of Genesis 1:26, which is a dominion not of domination but of stewardship, taking care of the world's back yard. Yet again, of course: God the world-maker is God the care-taker. Humans properly stand over other creatures only as they stand with other creatures, showing them love, giving them space, and granting them "rights." Humans are royally privileged, but *noblesse oblige*. Thus to be human is to be *ecological*. It is also, of course, to be *political*. Finally, insofar as we do as we are, we are *free*, for freedom—*libertas*—is not the freedom of "choice," which in fact is slavery, but the freedom for service.

7. To be human is to be *ludic*. Humans are the animal that plays and laughs. And—yet again—of course: because God plays and laughs. Creation itself is play, not work. On the first Sabbath God smiled—and partied! Eight-year-old Solveig is right, against her Poppi, that "Santa Claus is very much like God", because he is so "jolly."[2] And (in Umberto Eco's *The Name of the Rose*) the bespectacled Franciscan William is right, against the blind Dominican Jorge, that Jesus surely laughed, because he was fully human (tellingly, Jorge objects because laughter "convulses the body"—like sex). Indeed when humans laugh they ape the angels, who, as Chesterton said, "can fly because they take themselves lightly."

8. To be human is to be *doxological*. In Peter Shaffer's play *Equus* one of the characters says that if we don't worship, we shrink. Not to worship is spiritual desiccation. Worship is to the heart what water is to the tongue. Not that worship is *for* anything.

---

2. Robert W. Jenson and Solveig Lucia Gold, *Conversations with Poppi about God* (Grand Rapids, Michigan: Brazos Press, 2006), p. 28.

Worship, in fact, is totally useless. Indeed the question "Why worship God?" is a foolish one. "We worship God because God is to be worshipped";[3] indeed God, as Trinity, *is* worship. As service is the ultimate expression of our freedom before others, so worship is the ultimate expression of our freedom before God. It is also the ultimate expression of human *dignity*, "man well drest," as George Herbert imaged it; indeed "God's breath in man returning to his birth."

9. To be human is to be *Christ-like*. Indeed we are not truly human, only Christ is truly human, the iconic human, the image of God. Here is the truth in the Eastern concept of deification, better, perhaps, called *Christification*. We are human insofar as we are conformed to the image of Christ. Thus anthropology is a corollary of Christology—and staurology: *Ecce homo!* Thus baptism is the sacrament of humanity, because it is the sacrament of our death and resurrection in Christ (Romans 6:1–11)—and this is no metaphor! Through baptism, we become human beings—proleptically. Our being is in becoming—Christ.

10. To be human is to be *glorified*. Anthropology is Christology is eschatology, and eschatology is pneumatology: the Holy Spirit, the glorifier, is the perfecter of the human. If, with Moltmann, Pannenberg, and Jenson, the future is definitive of God's very being, so too with humans. So if, with Paul, we have died, and our "life is hidden with Christ in God" (Colossian 3:3), nevertheless so too with John, "what we will be has not yet been revealed" (I John 3:2). In trajectory towards the telos, we live by promise and hasten in hope, the heart of the human. In the end, the Father will put us on his knee and show us what we were really like—and who we really are: "we will be like him" (I John 3:2).

---

3. From the 1975 Hartford Appeal, cited in Ralph P. Martin, *The Worship of God* (Grand Rapids, Michigan: William B. Eerdmans, 1982), p. 4.

And all shall be well and
All manner of things shall be well
When the tongues of flame are in-folded
Into the crowned knot of fire
And the fire and the rose are one.
(T. S. Eliot, "Little Gidding", *Four Quartets*)

Holy Spirit, breath of life

Holy Spirit, breath of life,
 breathe upon me;
comforter in times of strife,
 make my fears flee.
You alone can save my soul
 from life's wild sea;
you alone can fill the hole
 deep within me.

Come, then, Spirit from above,
 fall upon me;
bond of Son and Father's love,
 set my soul free.
To the cell in which I'm bound
 you're the sole key;
through the years you've sought and found
 self-enclosed me.

God of warmth who goes between
 others and me;
God of light who can't be seen,
 help us to see:
only as we live in you
 can we then be;
living then for others too,
 I become me.

Ten Propositions on Freedom

1. An intellectual history of Europe since the Enlightenment could be written with the title "The Decline and Fall of the Concept of Freedom." The nadir has now been reached with the collapse of the modernist concept of freedom as "autonomy" into the postmodernist banality of freedom as "choice." From lifestyle and shopping, to schools and hospitals, to our bodies and death itself, the mantra is choice, choice, and more choice. Such a consumerist understanding of freedom suggests an isolated and empty ego walking with faux purpose through a mall, checking out the products as if a bargain were the meaning of life. It isn't. A more vulgar anthropology is hard to imagine.

2. Nor a more dangerous one: for "freedom of choice" read voracious appetite and will-to-power, the apotheosis of narcissism, the idolatry of the market, and the collapse of the common good into social nihilism. And all the more dangerous for the rhetorical force of the word "freedom," a "mom and apple pie" shibboleth, with its claim to ideological innocence and ethical obviousness, buttressed by the discourse of "rights" (which amount to fortifications of self-interest) and "tolerance" (which allows for difference only as tiresome variations of sameness). Here a hermeneutics of secular suspicion is de rigueur—but so too is a hermeneutics of theological retrieval and reconstruction.

3. Writing at the beginning of the Cold War, Isaiah Berlin famously plotted a pre- to post-Rousseau trajectory of freedom. Initially, Berlin referred to these two types of liberty as the "liberal" and the "romantic," the former understood as the absence of obstacles to thought and action, the latter understood as self-expression and -actualization. Later, in a seminal inaugural lecture at Oxford University in 1958, Berlin recast these concepts as "negative" and "positive" liberty. Berlin did not reject positive liberty as such, but he observed, historically, a "strange reversal": what began, for example in the French Revolution, as reformation ended in terror and tyranny.

4. Berlin was attacked from both left and right. The right resented his challenge to liberal elites and disputed his claim that the values of freedom and truth may be incompatible, and his insistence that liberty should therefore be disconnected from projects of liberation. The left argued that his critique of self-realization, while right about Rousseau, was a distortion of Kant and John Stuart Mill (whose own project had been the integration of the Enlightenment and Romanticism); and that while on target about Stalinism, it left laissez-faire regimes to run amok.

5. Needless to say, theologians must look on these internecine secular polemics with astonished detachment. The scene really is Pythonesque. How, we wonder, can these philosophers be unaware of the elephant in the room? Because, they think, the beast has long been banished to the Reservation for Otiose Deities. But why the enforced exile? Because they think that divine and human freedom is a zero-sum game, an exercise in irreducible agonistics. Because, in short, they have a pagan notion of divine omnipotence and presume the Trinity to be a mathematical nonsense.

6. Following Thomas Aquinas, Herbert McCabe writes: "God's activity, then, does not compete with mine. Whereas the activity of any other creature makes a difference to mine and would interfere with my freedom, the activity of God makes no difference. It has a more fundamental job to do than making a difference. It makes me have my own activity in the first place. I am free.... Not free of him (this would be to cease to exist), but free of other creatures. The idea that God's causality could interfere with my freedom can only arise from an idolatrous notion of God as a very large and powerful creature—a part of the world."[1]

---

1. Herbert McCabe, *Faith within Reason*, ed. Brian Davies (London: Continuum, 2007), pp. 75–76.

7. The inevitable and predictable upshot of this oppositional understanding of freedom is an antagonistic reading of human freedom over against nature, other individuals, society as a whole — and against God. And thus the concept of freedom as human autonomy, pre- or post-Rousseau, personal or political, is unmasked as destructive of the very liberty it purports to sustain. Indeed, with Orwellian irony, it amounts to a form of slavery. What we need is a non-competitive account of freedom, the freedom of the children of God, the freedom in which, by faith, we participate in God's own Trinitarian life. Paul writes: "Now the Lord is Spirit, and where the Spirit of the Lord is, there is freedom" (II Corinthians 3:17).

8. The starting point for such an account will be freedom as divine *gift*, the gift of me and the gift of others. I am free to be the unique person the Father has created me to be, freed by the Son from the false self I have become, enslaved to sin and death, freed for life in the Holy Spirit who perfects human freedom. The Trinity sets me free *from* self-concern, above all the self-concern of fear. But in the same dynamic movement, the Trinity sets me free *for* other people, given to me to love. True freedom is thus not any slack I am cut to do what I want. Evangelical freedom is the freedom to realize the person God calls me to be with the people God gives me to love.

9. Luther: "A Christian is a perfectly free lord of all, subject to none. A Christian is a perfectly dutiful servant, subject to all." The relationship between freedom and obedience is not antithetical but dialectical. Ben Quash suggests that Karl Barth "wants the creature to have the *obedient* embrace of *freedom*," while Hans Urs von Balthasar "wants the *free* embrace of *obedience*."[2] Both, however, are agreed that the free creature is

---

2. Ben Quash, "Exile, Freedom and Thanksgiving: Barth and Hans Urs von Balthasar", in John C. McDowell and Mike Higton (eds.), *Conversing with Barth* (Aldershot, England: Ashgate, 2004), p. 109.

characterized, above all, by joy and thanksgiving—and by prayer and praise.

10. Finally, a theological account of freedom must not only have a relational and social but also a *political* dimension, a baptized version of Berlin's positive liberty. The Old Testament paradigms are the exodus from Egyptian slavery and the return from Babylonian captivity. In the New Testament Jesus reconfigures Isaiah (not Berlin!) with his Jubilee manifesto (Luke 4:18–19, cf. Isaiah 61:1–2). The freedom of the children of God is more than political freedom, but its telos cannot be less than political freedom. When Western missionaries translated the Bible into African languages, for "redemption" they often used words that meant, literally, "God takes the chains from our necks." *Libertas* is a package deal—even if the package is finally unwrapped only in the *civitas Dei*.

Why do people go to church?

Why do people go to church?
   Why do we worship God?
While our neighbors lie in bed,
   why do we act so odd?
As we fold our hands and pray,
as we hear what preachers say,
as we pass around the tray,
   we would *become* the church.

Why do people go to church?
   Why do we get enthused?
While our neighbors work or play,
   why do we pack the pews?
As we sing our psalms and songs,
as we learn what's right and wrong,
as we try to get along,
   we would *become* the church.

Why do people go to church?
   Why do we offer praise?
While our neighbors sit in pubs,
   why do we stand amazed?
As forgiven we forgive,
as in gratitude we give,
as we practice how to live,
   we would *become* the church.

Here's why Christians come to church:
   because we've heard the call,
we're responding to the grace
   of God, the Lord of all.
We're not here because we choose,
we're not here to be amused,
we are here to hear Good News
   and so to *be* the church.

Ten Propositions on Worship

1. Why worship God? Because God is to be worshipped. Worship is a holy tautology.

2. Does worship make God present? No, worship presupposes God's presence. But God's presence is unlike any other. "God does not exist," said Kierkegaard, "he is eternal." Compared to all existents, God's presence is an absence. The Holy of Holies is empty. If worship is fundamentally eucharist, you could say that it is "thanks for nothing." Without this apophatic point of departure, worship inevitably becomes idolatrous.

3. Is worship necessary? Not for God it isn't. God does not need our worship because God *is* worship, the perichoretic adoration of Father, Son, and Holy Spirit. Worship is, however, necessary for us, for it is only as *homo adorans*, participating in the very life of the Holy Trinity, that we become truly human. We are not only social but also ceremonial animals.

4. Does worship please God? The question's assumption is right: God is the audience of worship, not the congregation (though you wouldn't know it from many a church service). But whether or not the audience approves depends. Worship pleases God when we wash our hands before we raise and fold them, that is, when our praise begins in penitence—and then issues in the politics of peace. Then we are all reading from the same hymn sheet. Otherwise see Amos 5:21–24.

5. How should worship begin? But worship never begins, or, rather, it has always already begun. You could say that we always arrive late for worship, because truly the service has always already started—the praise unceasing of the *communio sanctorum*, and of angels and archangels too. Never forget that when the church seems empty and there are only three old ladies and a dog in the pews (and all at the back!).

6. How should worship proceed? Worship is a dialogue, or, better, a two-beat tempo of revelation and response, grace and

gratitude. Worship is also an ellipse, spiralling around the foci of word and sacrament. And worship is a time machine that takes us back to the future. And the various liturgies? They are *aides-memoirs*, not incantations, synopses of the unfinished scripted (or, better, script-ured) story we are invited to indwell and improvise; therefore they should not aim at closure but make space for contemplation and imagination.

7. How should worship end? With an ellipsis ... For when the liturgy is over, the service (*leitourgia*) begins. Leaving the church is the ultimate liturgical act: *Ite, missa est.* On Romans 12:1–2, Ernst Käsemann observes that "the cultic vocabulary which [Paul] uses here serves a decidedly anti-cultic thrust." "Christian worship" he continues, "does not consist in what is practiced at sacred sites, at sacred times, and with sacred acts. It is the offering of bodily existence in the otherwise profane sphere."[1] Or as I once heard Bishop Michael Marshall say: "You do not become a Christian by sitting in the pew anymore than you become a car by sitting in the garage."

8. What should we get out of worship? Wrong question. Worship is not a utility but an offering, a sacrifice, an economy of grace that interrupts and critiques the feverish cycles of production and consumption—which is why the collection is not fund-raising but cultural critique. If you want relevance, excitement, or profit, go to a rally, a concert, or the stock exchange. To put it most counter-culturally: Blessed are the bored, for they will see God. Indeed you must be bored-again.

9. What about people who don't worship? We are responsible for them. Hence intercessions. But more: all worship is a vicarious act—in fact, Christ's vicarious act—so that when we come to worship, we bring the whole world with us. Without the world, we become an *ecclesia incurvata in se*. Worship is the

---

1. Ernst Käsemann, *Commentary on Romans* (London: SCM Press, 1980), p. 329.

end of "us" and "them"—and a sneak preview of the reconciliation of all things.

10. And what about worship as evangelism, education, ethics? Of course, but as the blessings, not the motives, of worship—blessings given as worship reconditions the habits of our hearts and reshapes our distorted characters.

Prayer the church's fast and feast

(In homage to the poem "Prayer" by George Herbert)

Prayer the church's fast and feast,
    recipes for grief and praise;
prayer the creature's common speech,
    mind and soul in paraphrase:

> *Father God, how good to share*
> *all our love and pain and care.*

Prayer the land of sun and spice,
    hearts on holiday abroad;
prayer the blood of sacrifice,
    blessed spear that pierced our Lord:

Prayer the compass of desire,
    pointing to the promised rest;
prayer the truth against the liar,
    passing all the devil's tests:

Prayer the token of the best,
    poetry of cheerful rhymes;
prayer the sound of deep unrest,
    thunderclaps for tempest-times:

Prayer the ear that hears the tones,
    sounding from angelic spheres;
prayer the voice that moves the stone,
    pressing on the tomb of years:

Prayer the raising of the dead,
    turning evil into good;
prayer the way the world is read,
    sense of something understood:

Ten Propositions on Prayer

1. There is no more outrageous and presumptuous idea than that we ought to be able to pray. Prayer is an impossible possibility. Prayer is miracle, prayer is resurrection from the dead. We pray not by nature but by grace. We are *free* to pray only as we are *freed* to pray. Only in Christ are we free: thus we pray *through* Jesus Christ our Lord.

2. Prayer, like play, is a completely useless activity, a total waste of time. To ask if prayer "works" is to reduce prayer to a mechanism and God to a utility, or, worse, to reduce prayer to a kind of magic and God to the Wizard of Oz. Eberhard Jüngel speaks of the "nonnecessity of God" (only the god of ontotheology is a necessary being; indispensability is not a predicate of the true God). God is not necessary, "God is more than necessary."[1] So, correspondingly, with prayer: prayer is not necessary, it is more than necessary.

3. We never begin to pray, we always enter prayer *in medias res*, prayer that has already begun before us and without us, the prayer of the church. We may pray alone, but we are never alone when we pray. Prayer is the end of the isolated ego: "*Our Father …*" A fortiori, what Wittgenstein says about thought goes for prayer: it is not a mental activity, something that goes on inside our heads, but a human action. Hence the importance of posture and gesture in prayer. And what is fasting but praying with your body?

4. Prayer is a risky, dangerous activity. The prie-dieu is
   … a plank
   to walk over seventy thousand fathoms,
   as Kierkegaard would say, and far out
   from the land.
   (R. S. Thomas, "Balance")

---

1. Eberhard Jüngel, *God as the Mystery of the World* (Edinburgh: T&T Clark, 1983), pp. 18, 24.

The experience of prayer is transformative. In prayer we are changed—and change is frightening and painful.

5. Even in private prayer goes public. Indeed prayer is the most *political* activity in which a Christian can engage. Political? Indeed *revolutionary*. "Thy kingdom come" is a call for the overthrow of all earthly governments. "To fold your hands in prayer is to begin an uprising against the world" (Karl Barth). Which is not an excuse for quietism. Augustine said, "Without God we cannot, without us God will not." *Ora et labora,* insisted the Reformers. Prayer and ethics belong together.

6. It is nonsense to suggest that prayers of adoration trump prayers of petition. We are children of God. What would you think of your own child if she never pestered you for things? You would think, "What an obnoxious little goody-goody." And we must be honest about what we want. In the film *Bruce Almighty*, Bruce (Jim Carrey) asks God (Morgan Freeman) how he's doing as he prays for justice and peace. "Fine," says God, "if you want to be Miss America. Now what do you really care about?" If we are honest with God about the small things, we can trust that he will lead us to the bigger things, especially the needs of others for whom we intercede.

7. With petition goes gratitude. What could speak more eloquently of our radical dependence on God than "Please" and "Thank you"? Yet prayer does not begin with the mouth, prayer begins with the eyes and ears. Prayer begins with *attentiveness*, with *listening*. Prayer begins with expectant *waiting* for a close encounter. Prayer is a date in which God makes the first move. "Surely some revelation is at hand" (W. B. Yeats, "The Second Coming").

8. It is also nonsense to ask whether or not God answers prayer. The Father is the object of prayer, the Spirit is the subject of prayer, the Son is the predicate of prayer. How then can God not answer his own prayers? If God is silent, it is because he is listening—and thinking about his answer. And as for those answers, William Temple said, "When I pray, coincidences

happen." Or not. The problem of unanswered prayer does not arise for Jesus. Yet the answer to his prayer in Gethsemane is "No." God is silent. This tells us something about prayer—and something about God.

9. Do you have arid times of prayer? Can't focus? Overwhelmed by distractions? Join the club! But flailing around in choppy seas, and even going under, gasping in the deep—that too is prayer. There are no points for poise or polish. And wherever did we get the idiotic and disabling idea that prayer must be a richly rewarding experience? From the Psalms we learn that lament as well as praise, cursing as well as blessing, can be prayer.

10. Ultimately, the question of prayer is the question of God: What kind of God do you believe in? Or better: *Who* is your God?

Where, we ask, is God today?

Where, we ask, is God today—
   in the gaps that science leaves,
   gaps that close as knowledge grows?
Such a God is on reprieve.

Where, we ask, is God today—
   in the private place of prayer,
   where we find security?
Such a God's a teddy bear.

Where, we ask, is God today—
   in the church, behind its walls,
   for a cause in quarantine?
Such a God is far too small.

Where, we ask, is God today—
   in jihad or cruel crusade,
   in the council room of war?
Such a God's the devil's aide.

Where, we ask, is God today—
   in the questions that we ask,
   in the puzzles and the pain?
God is in the toils and tasks!

Where, we ask, is God today—
   are we where his Christ would be,
   with the outcast and ignored?
Such is God's humanity!

Ten Propositions on Spirituality

1. "Spirituality" is a word suffering from runaway inflation. Let's try to stabilize the currency. Historical amnesia, false dichotomies, and fashionable therapies bedevil the subject.

2. Philip Sheldrake observes that the noun *spiritualitas* "only became established in reference to 'the spiritual life' in seventeenth century France — and not always in a positive sense," principally due to its clerical associations (in the Middles Ages the clergy *were* "the spirituality"). "It then disappeared from theological circles until the end of the nineteenth and beginning of the twentieth century when it again appeared in French in reference to the 'spiritual life'.... [B]ut it was only by the Second Vatican Council in the early 1960s that it began to dominate and replace older terms such as ascetical theology or mystical theology."[1] Then in the 1970s the term took off, and now, set to the key of the so-called New Age, spirituality has become the mood-muzak of postmodernity.

3. I've got nothing against psychology as such, but on the spirituality circuits that revolve around the gurus Myers-Briggs and James Fowler I often sense an approach to spirituality that lacks a "thick" Christian concept of the spirit (*pneuma*). At the very least it takes a semantic sleight of hand to reduce the "soul" to the "self" to the "personality," and to equate human potential and growth with sanctification, let alone to assume that in exploring ourselves we are exploring God the Holy Trinity. But then, as Alan Sell observes, "Christians, having swept their house clean of their native vocabulary, should not be unduly surprised if seven Carl Rogerses rush in to take its place."[2] By

1. Philip Sheldrake, *A Brief History of Spirituality* (Oxford: Blackwell, 2007), p. 3.
2. Alan Sell, *Nonconformist Theology in the Twentieth Century* (Milton Keynes, UK: Paternoster, 2006), p.179.

the way, for the life of me I do not understand how Christians
can prefer Jung to Freud as a theological resource (though it's
probably due to our preference for naivety to suspicion).

4. Theology without spirituality is empty, spirituality without
theology is blind. When theology is "thin," it is often because
it is not steeped in prayer; when spirituality is "lite," it is usually because it is theologically vacuous. Only in the West, and
only during the twelfth century, when the theological enterprise moved from the monasteries to the new universities, did
Christian thinking begin to become an activity distinct from *askesis* (spiritual "exercise"), while contemplation, in turn, tended
to become separate from both eucharist and ethics. Since the
High Middle Ages, Roman Catholics, and then Protestants
(Puritan, Anglican, and radically Reformed), have been working in different ways to stitch together what should be a seam-
less garment of the affective, the intellectual, and the active,
to reunite the speculative theologian and the practical saint.

5. Spirituality is theology with attitude, theology with soul—but
not a soul without a body. A truly Christian spirituality will be
incarnational—but it will not idolize health; and it will be cruciform—but it will not glorify pain. Fasting has been called
praying with your body, but feasting should be praying with
your body too. Biblically speaking, the opposite of *pneuma*
(spirit) is not *soma* (body) but *sarx* (flesh). Nor, needless to say,
are the "sins of the flesh" essentially sensual (cf. Galatians 5:19ff.).
Notwithstanding insidious Neo-Platonic, even Gnostic influence, a couple's bedroom as well as the monk's cell can be a
place where heaven and earth get it on (the Song of Songs' X-
rated eroticism is often lost through censored translation). In
fact, the material as such is (forgive the pun) a spiritual matter.

6. Spirituality has been called theology on its knees, but it is also
theology on its feet, in work as well as prayer. "Bread for myself is a physical matter," said Nikolai Berdyaev, "but bread for
my neighbor is a spiritual matter." Any authentic Christian spirituality will have *shalom*—peace-and-justice—at its heart.

Hans Urs von Balthasar said that "Whoever does not come to know the face of God in contemplation will not recognize it in action, even when it reveals itself to him in the face of the oppressed"[3]—but is not the reverse equally and emphatically true (Matthew 25:40, 45)? Dietrich Bonhoeffer famously wrote: "Only those who cry out for the Jews may sing Gregorian chant." It is no coincidence that liberation theologies are deeply committed to combining experience, reflection, action, and prayer/worship/eucharist.

7. So what is "spirituality"? Perhaps spirituality is one of those things that is easier to show than to say. If so, Rowan Williams, who sees thought itself as a practice of *askesis*, is the finest contemporary guide I know to what spirituality might look like, not least in his own personal and theological life. Williams suggests that we understand spirituality in terms of personal interrogative engagement with God, but he insists that spirituality is "far more than a science of interpreting exceptional private experiences; it must ... touch every area of human experience, the public and the social, the painful, negative, even pathological byways of the mind, the moral and relational world. And the goal of a Christian life becomes not enlightenment but wholeness—an acceptance of this complicated and muddled bundle of experiences as a possible theatre for God's creative work."[4]

8. In an important sense, then, "spirituality" is almost synonymous with *discipleship*, with starting from exactly where you are and taking the next step in following Jesus wherever he leads. Hence a good deal of holiness has to do with discernment, which requires *attendre* (Simone Weil), focused waiting and

3. Hans Urs von Balthasar, *Love Alone Is Credible* (San Francisco: Ignatius Press, 2004), p. 109.

4. Rowan Williams, *The Wound of Knowledge* (London: Darton, Longman and Todd, 1990 [first published in 1979]), p. 2.

concentration. Spirituality, then, as watchfulness, being alert
to the present moment, and, disabused of illusion and fantasy,
seeing what is really *there*—the toil to be truthful, the strug-
gle against self-deceit, the purification of desire. Unlike many
of the Pelagian nostrums on offer, Christian spirituality takes
sin seriously.

9. Authentic spirituality is an *exilic* practice, for nomads on a
journey. Thus the epigraph of the memoir *Practicing Exile*
(2002) by the American Jewish thinker Marc Ellis: "Exile, the
home I have with God; God, the home I have in exile." Peace
and perfection are redefined in terms of strain and growth,
what Gregory of Nyssa called *epektasis* (from Philippians 3:13).
To Augustine's famous image of the *cor inquietum* (restless
heart), add Gregory's image of the vertigo one feels at a cliff-
top, with the abyss below and the beckoning yet ever-receding
peaks beyond. Divine darkness and human incomprehension
become themes that will be explored in the night theology of
St. John of the Cross and the *theologia crucis* of Martin Luther.
We are a long way here from an easy spirituality of serenity
and happiness. We are not licking lollipops with some "inner
me," we are wrestling an angel at the Jabbok, and we come away
with a limp, not a trophy (Genesis 32:22–32). The wilderness
lies at the heart of Christian spirituality. In place of the New Age
bandwagon, the desert caravan.

10. "It was like waking from a dream of separateness, of spurious
self-isolation in a special world, the world of renunciation and
supposed holiness. The whole illusion of a separate holy existence is a dream.... This sense of liberation from an illusory difference [between monks and ordinary people] was such a relief
and such a joy to me that I almost laughed aloud."[5] Thus
Thomas Merton, a pioneer in explorations of ecumenical, inter-
faith, and ecological spiritualities, who yet knew that there is

---

5. Cited in Sheldrake, op. cit., p. 186.

no view from nowhere, no traditionless practice, no unmediated interiority, no silence unhaunted by speech (and no separation between spirituality and institutional religion, yet another trendy dichotomy that crumbles under scrutiny). In the end, if spirituality is about "me" at all, it is about my dispossession and transformation into a *proper* human being, my becoming a living hermeneutic of the Great Commandment, loving the Other and the other. As a saying attributed to the Desert Father known as John the Dwarf has it:

"You don't build a house by starting with the roof and working down. You start with the foundation."
They said, "What does that mean?"
He said, "The foundation is our neighbour whom we must win. The neighbour is where we start. Every commandment of Christ depends on this."[6]

---

6. Cited in Rowan Williams, *Silence and Honey Cakes: The Wisdom of the Desert* (Oxford: Medio Media, 2003), p. 25.

Church and World

We're the family of God

We're the family of God,
   and we are richly blessed
with traditions that are odd—
   including fancy dress!
But in Jesus we are one—
deacon, steward, priest, or nun—
though our journey's just begun
   to be the coming Church.

We are Baptist and Reformed,
   we're Catholic and Friend,
for there is no single norm,
   we need a special blend
to exalt and praise the Lord
in the silence, wine, and word—
but we sound a common chord
   to sing the coming Church.

As we gather here today
   to mark the Week of Prayer,
in commitment to the Way
   that leads from here to there,
may our worship well express
that the Christ whom we confess
is the goal to which we press
   to be the coming Church.

When our time together ends,
   it's then the service starts,
as the Holy Spirit sends
   us out to play our part:
may we hasten from this place
to the waiting human race
with the joyful news of grace,
   and be the coming Church.

Ten Propositions on Ecumenism

1. To adapt a famous saying of Emil Brunner, the church exists
by ecumenism as fire exists by burning. Church unity is not
an optional extra, or AOB on the parish or presbytery agenda,
or a responsibility that can be delegated to the ecumaniacs, it
is integral to MOAB, the ministry of *all* believers. Ecumenism
is not an ecclesial suggestion, it is a dominical command. Protestant and Catholic and Orthodox—we need each other, even if
as a conjunction of opposites. W. H. Auden suggested that "in
each of us, there is a bit of a Catholic and a bit of a Protestant;
for the truth is catholic, but the search for it is protestant."[1]
Above all, we must never assume that we know in advance the
nature of the unity we seek, otherwise ecumenism becomes a
matter of strategy and persuasion, or perhaps of communica-
tion and compromise, when we should expect disruption and
recreation. Unity is an eschatological concept.

2. In his Farewell Discourse in John, Jesus asks the Father to sanc-
tify his disciples in the truth as he sends them into the world.
Then he prays: "I ask not only on behalf of these, but also on
behalf of those who will believe in me through their word, that
they may be one. As you, Father, are in me, and I am in you,
may they also be in us, so that the world will believe that you
have sent me" (John 17:20–21). The ecumenical imperative is
inherent in the missionary imperative. How can the church,
with integrity, proclaim *shalom* to the world when we are not
a truly catholic *koinonia*? And our catholicity must be recog-
nizably *visible*; a merely "spiritual" unity is a form of ecclesial
docetism.

3. And speaking of *koinonia* and *shalom*: consider the cases of
Martin Niemöller and John Howard Yoder. Niemöller said, "Be-

---

1. Cited in Arthur Kirsch, *Auden and Christianity* (New Haven: Yale University Press, 2005), p. 109.

cause I was an ecumenist, I became a pacifist," while Yoder observed that the ecumenical movement has its roots not only in the mission field but also in the peace movement. However my intention is not only to draw attention to the connection between unity and non-violence, my more general point is this: orthopraxy should be as integral to the ecumenical project as orthodoxy. After all, in the New Testament unity in ethics is no less central than unity in doctrine. It is a mistake to see unity as a circle with ecclesiology at the center; it is rather an ellipse with two foci, Faith and Order and Church and Society—not the one without the other. The old adage "doctrine divides, service unites" inscribes a false, fragmented understanding of unity, because doctrine and service are intrinsically indivisible.

4. Nor can faith and order issues be reduced to a checklist where churches tick the boxes. Which leads to the question: Do you think of Christian unity primarily in terms of consensus to be reached, or *koinonia* to be received and witness to be shared? If the former, it would not be surprising if you were indifferent to ecumenism—indeed you would be right to be so: unity-as-consensus is always but a hair's breadth from a kind of works righteousness. We are called not to agree with each other but to love one another. Proper structures of Christian unity will not only tolerate dissent, they will encourage it, and be forums for it. Whatever we may mean by or envisage about the "world church," it cannot be an ecclesial simulacrum of globalization.

5. We are called to be one because God is one. But the one God is Trinity: that is why unity cannot mean uniformity. The watchword of ecclesial diversity can sometimes give the impression that it is simply a tactical ploy to appease Christians who value freedom of conscience and fear centralized authority. On the contrary, it issues from the very nature of God (though it is hazardous to venture direct correspondences from the Trinity to ecclesial pluriformity). And scholars as denominationally different as Ernst Käsemann, James Dunn, and Raymond Brown confirm that the New Testament itself canonically sanctions a

variety of forms of Christianity. There are, of course, limits to acceptable diversity, but I would suggest that they lie within the parameters of: (a) a common baptism, (b) a Trinitarian confession of faith, and (c) a belief in Christ crucified and risen as Lord and Savior. All else are *adiaphora*—particularly matters of polity. Moreover, it would be unreasonable to expect more agreement between our churches than we accept within our churches.

6. And *episcopacy*? There is no question about *espicopé* (oversight) as such. The question is *mono-episcopacy*. The question is complicated by what John Webster rightly calls naive accounts of apostolic succession—"their incapacity to envisage the history of episcopacy as political and ideological."[2] And non-episcopal churches, of course, cannot accept that mono-episcopacy is the *esse* of the church—the ascended, ruling Christ alone, the one high priest (Hebrews) and *episcopos* of our souls (I Peter 2:25), is the *esse* of the church. But that does not prevent us from being open to mono-episcopacy as the *practical*, rather than *constitutive*, *bene esse* of the church, along the lines of what Calvin called "convenience," and what we might call "practical reason." The crucial question is: Does mono-episcopacy best witness to the ministry of Christ in his church, and best serve the apostolic project of *missio Spiritus*? Anglicans and Lutherans—as well as non-episcopal churches—have recently shown some movement on questions concerning the nature of episcopacy and the reconstruction of the episcopate. Of course if Rome pursues the Frank Sinatra school of ecumenism—"I did it my way"—the future is bleak. But you know the old saying: at the next Vatican council the bishops will bring their wives—and at the one after that they will bring their husbands!

7. An even more promising suggestion that relativizes the issue of mono-episcopacy comes from the nineteenth century Wes-

---

2. John Webster, *Word and Church: Essays in Christian Dogmatics* (Edinburgh: T&T Clark, 2001), p. 210.

leyan ecclesiologist Benjamin Gregory. Commenting on the visit of Peter and John to new Christian communities in Samaria (as David Carter writes), Gregory observed that "whenever they found the work of the Spirit, the apostles lost no time in recognising, receiving, and connecting that which had been established independently of their own initiative." Which insight led Gregory to a doctrine of *apostolic recognition*: namely, that "it should be the duty of the leaders of any church that claims ... a genuine apostolic continuity to recognise the preservation ... of Christianity under whatever forms and structures it may find."[3] And a doctrine of apostolic recognition, it seems to me, entails, at least, a generous approach to eucharistic hospitality. As Paul tells the divided church at Corinth, it is not because there is one body that there is one loaf, just the reverse: because there is one loaf, there is one body. The fraction prohibits faction. Ultimately, apostolic recognition rests on the acknowledgement that our unity is in Christ alone.

8. Of course it is not only conservative Catholics who can frustrate ecumenical initiatives, conservative evangelicals can be equally obstructive. The card they usually play is that truth trumps unity, and they are fond of citing Ephesians 4:15ff. George Caird, however, comments on "speaking the truth in love": "Paul is not recommending frankness of speech tempered by consideration, nor is he suggesting that the claims of *truth* and *love* must be held in some sort of tension. There is no Christian *truth* which is not 'rooted and grounded in love,' and *love* is the only legitimate test of men's adherence to the truth of the gospel.... Those who perpetuate the divisions of Christendom on the grounds of their loyalty to truth can draw no support from this epistle."[4] Or as I once heard a Catholic

---

3. David Carter, "Where Are We Ecclesiologically?" (March 1999), a paper prepared for the Theology and Unity Group of Churches Together in England.

4. George Caird, *Paul's Letters from Prison* (Oxford: Oxford University Press, 1976), p. 77.

theologian expound I Corinthians 13: unity of charity trumps unity of faith.

9. In my view, perhaps the greatest obstacle to an ecumenical future is the refusal to acknowledge our anti-ecumenical pasts. Catholics have killed Protestants, and Protestants have killed Catholics—indeed Protestants have killed other Protestants. I submit that progress in unity will be a pseudo-progress, a movement in historical denial, unless we engage in specific, collective, and mutual acts of penitence, forgiveness, and pledges of "Never again!" Only with the healing of memories can the church proceed in a pilgrimage of hope and promise. Moreover, unless the ministry of the whole people of God moves to the center of ecumenical discussions still overwhelmingly preoccupied with the convergence of ordained ministries, the church of the future, like the church of the past, will still have the *laos* taking up the rear of a convoy led by the *kleros*. And, of course, repentance, recognition, and reconciliation are only staging posts on the ecumenical journey: there is an elephant in the caravan and its name is Israel. And journey's end is the whole *oikoumene*.

10. Finally, a confession: I am part of the ecumenical problem, not its solution. The fact of the matter is that ecumenical work always seems to depend on church leaders, the men at the top—and they usually are men—working at the national or international level, while Christians at the grassroots—who are predominantly women—are marginalized and patronised. Moreover, our discussions tend to focus on deracinated ideas, divorced from their social location and unrelated to questions of ideology and power. They are also often off the pace of hermeneutical developments—and, crucially, contemporary biblical theology. The recent Common Statement by Lutherans and Roman Catholics on the doctrine of justification, for example, "ecumenical breakthrough" though it may be, takes little account of the "new perspective on Paul" that has been reconfiguring New Testament studies since the 1970s. Dog-

matic theologians are now rightly expected to be fluent ex-
egetes; we should expect no less from ecumenical theologians.
With regular, informed, and prayerful meeting around the
Word in local communities, which are the beating hearts of
ecumenism, dry bones may yet be knit together and live.

Postscript: a Joke

The Trinity was discussing their summer holidays. The Father said,
"I think I'll go somewhere in Africa again this year. The Africans are
still so patriarchal; unlike the Europeans, they make me feel important. What about you, Son?" The Son said, "I'm going to
Jerusalem again. I know last year the mayor tried to get me to pick
up the unpaid tab for the last supper, but the people treat me special, and the hotels give me five-star service." "What about you?"
the Father and the Son asked the Holy Spirit. The Holy Spirit replied:
"I'm thinking Rome this year: I've never been there before." (For Rome,
feel free to substitute Geneva, Wittenberg, Constantinople, Can-
terbury ...)

~

Imagine a world

Imagine a world where our leaders aren't liars,
    distorting reporting and spinning the news;
where all whistle-blowers and brave Jeremiahs
    are lauded, applauded, and never abused.

Imagine a world where believers aren't fighting
    and shedding our blood in the name of their gods;
where faith is delightful, enlightening, inviting,
    and never deployed for crusades or jihads.

Imagine a world where the markets aren't idols,
    bowed down to and worshipped in envy and greed;
where wealth is released and the bankers are bridled,
    the poor have a plot and the famished a feed.

Imagine a world where there is no pollution,
    the air is so clear and the oceans are clean;
where humans don't threaten the earth's evolution,
    the animals flourish and forests are green.

Imagine a world as the Lord has intended,
    where goodness and justice and beauty preside;
a world we have broken that might yet be mended:
    the future is now, it is ours to decide.

Ten Propositions on Political Theology

1. The doctrine of the ascension is the basis of all political theology—and why there can be no such thing as apolitical theology. The church cannot be a *cultus privatus* because Jesus of Nazareth, "crucified under Pontius Pilate," is Lord. The cross is a coup, the resurrection a coronation, and the ascension a triumphal procession. The gospel is public truth. Remove Christ from the *forum* and it does not remain empty: nature abhors a vacuum; idols love one and soon fill it.

2. God is political. Cut the political bits out of the Bible—as Jim Wallis and some friends once did—and you're left with "a Bible full of holes." God is political—and God does not wear a blindfold, God takes sides. In the Old Testament, Yahweh's exodus and covenant "preferential option for the poor" is now a well-worn phrase—but an undeniable fact. And the New Testament—Luke in particular—doesn't drop the ball: the Magnificat and the Jubilee Manifesto suggest the game plan. However if, as liberation theologians insist, the tree of peace has justice for its roots, it can blossom only in the soil of forgiveness: if peace without justice is conflict in denial, justice without forgiveness is vengeance with an easy conscience.

3. In my view it is legitimate to speak of an "epistemological privilege" of the excluded and oppressed. Bonhoeffer, writing in prison, was *avant la lettre* of liberationists: "We have for once learnt to see the great events of world history from below, from the perspective of the outcast, the suspects, the maltreated, the powerless, the oppressed, the reviled—in short, from the perspective of those who suffer." Here is the "more rewarding principle for exploring the world in thought and action than personal good fortune."[1]

---

1. Dietrich Bonhoeffer, *Letters and Papers from Prison* (London: SCM Press, 1971 [first published in 1953]), p. 17.

4. With a shrug of their shoulders, conservatives love to quote the text, "You always have the poor with you" (Mark 14:7), as if poverty were an order of creation (cf. "the rich man in his castle,/the poor man at his gate"), so that there is nothing we can — or should — do about it. But Jesus was not being cynical, or even realistic, about the inevitability of an excluded underclass, rather he was reminding his disciples where *they* will be found if they are faithful — ministering among the poor and oppressed.

5. The point is not that the poor and oppressed have a monopoly on virtue, let alone that they are an elect group, rather it is simply that they are the ones who get screwed — and God doesn't like people getting screwed. So God sends his servant Moses, his spokesmen the prophets, and finally his Son Jesus, their Big Brother, to take care of the bullies, though he fights with his mouth not his fists. Not, of course, that God loves the oppressor any less than he loves the oppressed; indeed his rescue mission is to liberate them both, the latter from their humiliation and suffering, and the former from their vanity and violence.

6. Nor does any political theologian who is not a straw man hold the Marxist delusion that utopia can be built, the fantasy of Babel. Karl Barth, responding to a theological student who had heard him lecture, wrote: "Many thanks for your kind letter. But ... now you manage to put down on paper again all that nonsense about the kingdom of God that we must build. Dear N.N., in so doing you do not contradict merely one 'insight' but the whole message of the whole Bible. If you persist in this idea I can only advise you to take up any other career than that of pastor."[2] The antidote to political Pelagianism is a critical eschatology. Barth himself was, of course, no quietist. He in-

---

2. Karl Barth, in Jürgen Fangmeier and Hinrich Stoevesandt (eds.), *Karl Barth: Letters: 1961–1968* (Edinburgh: T&T Clark, 1981), p. 283.

sisted that a community that observed the events of its day from the sideline, that kept its mouth shut and refused to dirty its hands, could not possibly be the church of Jesus Christ.

7. Still, calling governments to account and repentance, the critical component, and praying and working for a community of *shalom* and an economy of grace, the positive component, are essential elements of the political vocation of the church. Strategically Christians should work for a world which asymptotically approaches the kingdom of God. Tactically Christians should form ad hoc alliances and coalitions with all people of good will to spearhead adroit and resourceful political interventions in pursuit of the common good. Jesus said: "Whoever is not against us is for us" (Mark 9:40). And William Blake said: "What is now proved was once only imagined."

8. The flipside of an apolitical church is a sacralized state. This is the Constantinian heresy, fuelled by myths of exceptionalism. And a sacralized state easily becomes a demonic state. The cross is draped with the flag, and discipleship is absorbed into a patriotism that asks no questions. The German Christians are the paradigmatic nationalist idolaters; tragedy repeats itself in the farce of the Religious Right. "Never was anything in this world loved too much," wrote Thomas Traherne, "but many things have been loved in a false way." Christians are resident aliens, "our citizenship (*politeuma*) is in heaven" (Philippians 3:20): the love of Christ transcends the love of country.

9. The basis of a responsible and effective political theology is a robust ecclesiology. The church's political witness ends in the public square, but it begins in local congregational polity, around a pulpit and a table. At worship the church bows neither to Caesar (nation), nor to Mars (militarism) or Mammon (capitalism), but to the crucified and risen Lord. Because radical values and activism are not enough, at worship the Spirit begins to reshape our disordered desires—particularly assertions of coercive power—and teach us the arts of generosity and

forgiveness. Yet worship can be a bolthole rather than a sign of resistance. "Where the body is not properly discerned, Paul reminds the Corinthians, consumption of the Eucharist can make you sick or kill you (1 Cor. 11.30). This might explain the condition of some of our churches."[3]

10. The Apocalypse of John is an imaginative theological mural, luridly colored, depicting a fledgling church under attack from the mighty eagle of Rome, but its encoded message is perennially suggestive—and explosive. It is a samizdat text of protest to the pretensions of power, a warning against complacency, and a call to discernment in reading the signs of the times. The powerful inevitably twist it into a self-serving mandate for acquisition and aggression; only those who long for justice and peace see that the hermeneutical key is the slaughtered Lamb who gently roars. Here is the text for a political theology that begins to re-imagine and re-direct the world in anticipation of the parousia of Christ.

Post-9/11 Postscript

In *Apocalypse Now: Reflections on Faith in a Time of Terror* (2005), Duncan Forrester proposes an interesting juxtaposition: on the one hand, the statement of support for the Kaiser published by a group of ninety-three leading German intellectuals, including theologians, on the day the First World War broke out; on the other hand, the public "Letter from America: What We Are Fighting For" in support of President Bush's "war on terror," signed by sixty prominent American intellectuals, including theologians, five months after 9/11. Both letters are so theologically thin, however, that they amount to pom-pom propaganda for imperial states. The first letter awoke Karl Barth from his Schleiermacherian slumbers, the second aroused Stanley Hauerwas and Paul Griffiths to a polemical response. But

---

3. William T. Cavanaugh, *Theopolitical Imagination* (London: T&T Clark, 2002), p. 121.

by and large the people of Germany and the US sleepwalked into slaughter. Moral: When political theology is faithful, expect it to be critical and subversive; when it is unfaithful, expect it to be ideological and fatal.

O God of peace

O God of peace, whose peace is Christ your Son,
put on your armor that the war be won,
the war on war, your Word against the gun:
    Allelulia! Allelulia!

O God of power, whose power appears so weak,
call up your soldiers from among the meek,
who won't turn tail, but turn the other cheek:
    Allelulia! Allelulia!

O God of love, whose love casts out all fear,
steady your people when the warlike jeer,
but rather insults than their blood and tears:
    Allelulia! Allelulia!

O God of hosts, whose host is bread for life,
feed us by faith for strength in times of strife,
and fill with hope the grieving child and wife:
    Allelulia! Allelulia!

O God of time, whose time is always nigh,
keep us alert to leaders' lethal lies,
come now your reign when truth will never die:
    Allelulia! Allelulia!

Ten Propositions on Peace and War

1. God is the God of peace. The Father, as the *fons bonorum* (the fount of all goodness), is the source of peace; the Son, of course, is the Prince of Peace; and the Spirit, as the *vinculum caritatis* (bond of love) between the Father and the Son, is the Spirit of peace. To re-phrase I John 1:5: God is non-violent, and in him there is no violence at all. Here is the theological basis of an ontology, an epistemology, and an ethics of peace.

2. Is this a tendentious use of scripture? Not at all. Christian theology is trinitarian precisely because it is Christocentric. The Jesus disclosed in the New Testament preached and practiced non-violence—no if's, and's, or but's. This Jesus said, "Whoever has seen me has seen the Father" (John 14:9). Indeed he said, "The Father and I are one" (John 10:30). He also said, "The Holy Spirit, whom the Father will send in my name, will teach you everything, and remind you of all that I have said to you" (John 14:26)—and then immediately: "Peace I leave with you; my peace I give to you. I do not give to you as the world gives" (John 14:27).

3. And the "awkward" New Testament texts? The "sword" in Matthew 10:34 is clearly a metaphor for the conflict that the mission of Jesus provoked; while the "sword" in Luke 22:36 which Jesus tells the disciples to buy—when? where?—is surely ironic. As for the Cleansing of the Temple, it is hardly a political manifesto but rather an enacted parable ("street theater" it's been called) in the venerable tradition of prophetic symbolism. And Romans 13:1–5? In fact early Christian martyrs used these verses to declare their loyalty to Caesar—at the moment of their executions! Presumably it had not escaped their attention that Romans 13:1–5 happens to be preceded by Romans 12:14–21. There is no support whatsoever in Paul's letters for Christians engaging in violence. And in the rest of the New Testament, including Revelation, military imagery is deconstructed and deployed in the service of peace: the Lion of Judah goes "Baaa!" (Revelation 5:5–6).

4. And the Lord of Hosts of the Old Testament? Two points. First, the tradition of Holy War gets its purchase only in the context of the ritual purity of Israel, which makes the "ethnic cleansing" of the Canaanites a phrase that is historically apt, but an episode that is now quite irrelevant, not to say even in its time abhorrent. And second, because it was said to be Yahweh who led the troops in Israel's wars, the Holy War tradition functioned as a divine denunciation, not endorsement, of militarization. In any case, the non-violence of Jesus trumps the war cries of Israel's judges and kings. And given the clarity of the dominical example and teaching, which are so revolutionary yet so indisputable, accusations of Marcionism are the last refuge of the exegetical scoundrel. If angelic armies once bore weapons and cried, "Over the top!", now they now join hands, play (mouth) organs, and sing, "We shall overcome!"

5. Of course the church has honored the Sermon on the Mount more in the breach than the observance. The Sermon provides "counsels of perfection" (the medieval church), or it is inapplicable in the secular realm (Luther), or it is an "interim ethic" (Albert Schweitzer), or an impossible ideal (Reinhold Niebuhr — who, by the way, conceded that "The ethic of Jesus is uncompromisingly pacifist"). But although, say, Matthew 5:38–48 is illustrative rather than exhaustive, it is clearly meant to be followed by the entire Christian community — and followed to the letter. But, more, it is spoken to the world — Christian morality is never sectarian — as Matthew 28:20 makes absolutely clear. Observe too the placement of the sixth and final antithesis regarding the love of enemies — it is the radicalization of the first and the climax of the lot. Declared from a height, it is the Everest of ethics.

6. And so-called Just War theory? It is the Trojan horse in the city of God. If ever there was a knockdown incrimination against natural theology this is it. Its origins lie in Stoicism, the pinnacle of philosophy in the Pax Romana — which, of course, is spin for "imperial terror." Augustine (who, in fact, was less than

satisfied with the implications of his own teaching) acted in haste—and ever since the church has been repenting at leisure. (Hastiness is the characteristic vice of non-pacifism.) Just War theory is the elephant in the confessional, the bad faith of the church. Its intentions are no doubt good—but then we all know what the way to hell is paved with.

7. And even if there were once a time when a case could be made for the plausibility of Just War theory, that day is long gone. WMD—and the impossibility of meeting the *jus in bello* criteria of proportionality and discrimination—have ensured that only casuistry, and the extremely problematical principle of double-effect, can save it And George W. Bush's so-called "war on terror" has all but terminally discredited Just War casuistry—by the contempt for international treaties and conventions, by the displacement of the more precise principle of *pre-emptive* strike in response to an *immediate* threat with the vaguer principle of *preventative* warfare, by the staggering failure to plan an exit strategy and prepare for *jus post bellum*, and by the repugnant justification of the torture of prisoners. Just War theory is a busted flush. Once again, but now more than ever, Christians must ask themselves whether it is only as conscientious objectors that they can bear a faithful and credible witness to Jesus Christ in a violent world.

8. Time to return to our roots. For its first two hundred-plus years the church was pacifist. "Christ," wrote Tertullian (c. 160–c. 225), "in disarming Peter, disarmed every soldier"—and Tertullian's words are echoed by Irenaeus, Clement, Origen, Cyprian, Lactantius, Maximillian, Marcellus, et. al. Some scholars suggest that early Christian pacifism had more to do with the prohibition on taking oaths to the emperor than with the non-violence of Jesus, but given the weight of patristic evidence, not to mention the centrality of Christ's command to love our enemies, that hardly seems likely. In any case, pacifist—*radically* pacifist—the church was until (you guessed it!) the "nationalization" and domestication of the church under Con-

stantine. Ever since, mainline churches — Just War theory
notwithstanding — have consistently given their blessing to
wars fought by the empire or nation in which they resided.

9. Time to return to our roots — and to heed the faithful witness
of the historic peace churches (like the Waldensians, the An-
abaptists, and the Quakers). Karl Barth was right when he said
that the case for pacifism is almost overwhelmingly strong.
And it should be remembered that while Barth allowed for
war — non-nuclear war — in exceptional, borderline, limiting
cases, Barth's critique of war is devastating and quite unique in
the history of Protestant political thought. With Barth, the
possibility of engaging in war hangs by a thread — and if you
want to see even that thread cut, check out John Howard Yoder,
Karl Barth and the Problem of War (1970). I am a mere mon-
key: Yoder is *the* organ grinder. Even Stanley Hauerwas — as
he would fully agree — is not fit to untie Yoder's Hushpuppies.

10. "But pacifism is so impractical!" As if Christian ethics were
utilitarian, as if there were a calculus for *shalom*! "Get real! We
live in a sinful world." As if the "damage limitation" of Just War
theory, *precisely* given our sinful world, were realistic! "For the
Christian, a realistic apprehension of the world does not consist in factual survey and surmise, but in an evaluative reading of its signs as *clues to ultimate meanings and causes*,"[1] a
reading framed by the Christian narrative, by the crucifixion
and resurrection of Jesus, the hinge event for Christian pacifists, and the reason why, ultimately, the debate turns on eschatology. In any case, it is not as if the whole church has tried
pacifism and found it wanting, the fact is that the *whole* church
has not tried pacifism at all. But let Hauerwas have the last
word. "Nonviolence," he states, "is not one among other be-
havioral implications that can be drawn from the gospel but
is integral to the shape of Christian convictions.... Indeed,

---

1. John Milbank, "The Poverty of Niebuhrianism", in *The Word Made
Strange* (Oxford: Blackwell, 1997), p. 244.

nonviolence is not just one implication among others that can be drawn from our Christian beliefs; it is at the very heart of our understanding of God."[2] And, pulling no punches: "If we do not think it possible to love our enemies then we should plainly say Jesus is not the messiah."[3] But he is! Therefore, as friends and followers of Jesus, because we *may* love our enemies, we *must* love our enemies.

Ten Stations on My Way to Christian Pacifism

1. I graduated from Huntington High School (New York) in 1966 and Wesleyan University in 1970. The Cold War and the nuclear arms race; the brutal reactions to the Civil Rights Movement and racial integration; the assassinations of the Kennedy brothers, and of Malcolm X and Martin Luther King; the executions of Caryl Chessman and Adolf Eichmann; the riots in Watts, Detroit, Newark, and other major American cities; the war in Vietnam; the shootings at Kent State: these images of death were an inescapable and invasive reality of the years of my youth, even though my rather privileged upbringing provided a shelter, if not a bolthole, from the storm.

2. At Wesleyan I majored in English. My teachers included Ihab Hassan and Richard Slotkin. Hassan, through Freud and Norman O. Brown, introduced me to the psychic god Thanatos (Death); Slotkin, through his work on the myth of the Amer-

---

2. Stanley Hauerwas, *The Peaceable Kingdom: A Primer in Christian Ethics* (Notre Dame, Indiana: University of Notre Dame Press, 1983), p. xvii.

3. Stanley Hauerwas, "September 11, 2001: A Pacifist Response", in Stanley Hauerwas and Frank Lentricchia (eds.), *Dissent from the Homeland: Essays after September 11* (North Carolina: Duke University Press, 2003), pp. 191f.

ican frontier, to our national god Mars: violence—its appropriation and legitimation so central to American self-identity. *The Power of Blackness*, the title of Harry Levin's classic study of the leitmotif running through the fiction of Melville, Hawthorne, and Poe, sums up the Augustinian take on the human condition that was shaping my spiritual formation, for, pagan that I was, the *Confessions* too had made a powerful intellectual impact.

3. And then there was Joseph Conrad's *Heart of Darkness*: I discovered that Kurtz's heart was *my* heart. Although all through adolescence I never got into fistfights, I was aware of an aggressive streak running like a coal seam through my character, safely, indeed rewardingly, sublimated into a fierce competitiveness in study and sport. "The horror! The horror!" of it only became deeply personal during several ugly experiences at the tail end of the sixties and the spring of 1970. The grim months between the murders of King and Bobby Kennedy and the invasion of Cambodia were a national nadir that aptly coincided with my sense of self-defeat and depression.

4. Eventually Jesus Christ, armed only with his word, launched his attack on me, and, exposing my situation as infinitely more hopeless than I had ever suspected, rescued me from behind enemy lines—though to this day I continue to skirmish and resist. As, of course, does the world. It never occurred to me that, with the peace of God, the personal isn't the political—and vice-versa. II Corinthians 5:16–19 was a key text as I headed off to the University of Oxford for my ministerial training. While Martin Luther King was a role model (his collection of sermons *Strength to Love* was inspirational), it was above all Karl Barth to whom I turned during my three years at Mansfield College, as I tried to think through and work out a personal and political theology that I could live—and preach.

5. Barth seriously engaged the ethics of war and considered the case for pacifism to be almost irresistibly persuasive. However Barth rejected "absolute" pacifism, allowing for what he called

the *Grenzfall*, the exceptional case, where war-making is not only permitted but commanded. While Barth himself did not directly cite classical just war theory (not surprisingly given his rejection of casuistry, not to mention the theory's origins in the philosophy of natural law), nevertheless I had enough respect for Augustine, Aquinas, and modern revisionists, and sufficient scruple about the staple example of the Second World War, to factor it into my thinking. Result: about the time of my ordination in 1982, I was an "almost pacifist."

6. Nuclear pacifism was a whistle stop. In the face of WMD, just war theory buckled and collapsed. I am proud to say that my own United Reformed Church (UK) passed a resolution on unilateral nuclear disarmament by a two-thirds majority at its 1983 General Assembly—a position, alas, not reflected in local congregations where the realpolitik idol of deterrence was—and is—widely worshipped. Such grass roots Reformed recalcitrance, and the dithering of the Church of England, as well as Margaret Thatcher's rout of the Labour Party in the 1983 General Election (Labour's election manifesto was unilateralist—and was dubbed "the longest suicide note in history"), only hardened my resolve and drove me further to radicalize my thinking.

7. I should say that at no time did I have any truck with two kingdoms doctrine, in spite of clarifications and fine-tuning by theologians like Pannenberg. My thoroughly Reformed understanding of the universal Lordship of Christ over church and world (or state) precluded any such Lutheran "compromises." As for Niebuhr's Christian "realism," theological "stoicism" is more like it: paper-thin doctrines of the Spirit and the church, issuing in a cynical attitude towards sanctification and regeneration, and behind it all a mythological interpretation of the resurrection of Christ. On the other hand, Reformed theology (pace Barth) gave little guidance to my developing pacifism. Ironically, here it took a Lutheran to keep me on the straight and narrow—and a Mennonite to take me the rest of the way.

8. The Lutheran was Dietrich Bonhoeffer. I had already discovered and dismissed the four traditional interpretations of the Sermon on the Mount: as a "counsel of perfection," reserved for the monastery; as a "mirror of sin" (Luther's *usus pedagogicus legis*), driving us to despair and the *sola fide*; as an "impossible ideal," inspiring us to high moral endeavor; and as an apocalyptic "interim ethic" (the thesis of Johannes Weiss and Albert Schweitzer). However it took Bonhoeffer, in *The Cost of Discipleship*, to resurrect the perfectionist conception—what he called the "extraordinary"—only now understood as gospel, not law, and for all disciples, not just the few. It was also Bonhoeffer who taught me to take "activist non-violence" (Ronald Sider), which he admired in Ghandi and would be deployed to such effect by Martin Luther King, not just as a tactical ethic, the answer to the "realist" utopian critique, but as a divine command to be obeyed irrespective of results.

9. The Mennonite, of course, was John Howard Yoder (with a nod to the then Methodist Stanley Hauerwas as a sandal-bearer). The Christology of *The Politics of Jesus* deepened my *imitatio Christi* pacifism and added a participatory and eschatological context, with resurrection power, to its cruciform shape. Yoder's kingdom-centered ecclesiology combined with his ecumenical vision re-energized my commitment to a Just Peace Church. Then *Karl Barth and the Problem of War* pinpointed several major inconsistencies in Barth's ethics of war, suggested a failure in Barth's theological nerve as well as in his political imagination, and resolved any lingering suspicions that Christian pacifism might be a hubristic occlusion, rather than an obedient expression, of the freedom of God.

10. Finally, if Christian pacifism has—and it has—its basis in Jesus, the non-violent one whose power is perfected in weakness, and if Jesus is—and he is—the human hermeneutic of God, and, further, if theological construction begins with the economic Trinity and works back to the immanent Trinity as its eternal source and substantiation—in short, if God is non-violent,

and in him there is no violence at all—then, clearly, not only urgent ethical, but also major doctrinal reconfigurations are in order, not least in soteriology, which should be very high, as a pacifist's Christology should be very high. And pneumatology too. And that takes me back to me—the violent me, the reluctantly peaceful me, the me so suitably equipped, therefore, for pacifism. Because (purloining Barth), pacifism is an impossible possibility, and because (purloining Jüngel) pacifism is not necessary but more than necessary, at the heart of Christian pacifism lies prayer, the prayer: "*Veni, Creator Spiritus!*"

Postscript

There is, of course, no single variety of Christian pacifism, and several typologies have been suggested delineating various historical and normative positions. David L. Clough and Brian Stiltner provide a helpful classification in *Faith and Force: A Christian Debate about War* (Georgetown University Press, 2007). In their "scales," my own brand of Christian pacifism is *principled* rather than (merely) *strategic* (calculative and consequentialist); *classical* rather than *absolute* (the former allowing for legitimate domestic and, in theory, international policing functions, the latter entailing anarchism); *politically engaged* rather than *separatist*; and *universal* in intent rather than (merely) *communal* (because Christ is Lord not just of the church but of the world).

In Christ we're neither nor

In Christ we're neither nor,
    for all in Christ are one;
Christ is himself the open door
    through whom the nations come.

In Christ nor Greek nor Jew,
    as oppositions fall
before the one who twins the two
    by breaking down the wall.

In Christ nor slave nor free,
    now all are slaves to each,
and equal in his company
    the greatest and the least.

In Christ nor he nor she,
    so men may now be meek,
while women hold apostles' keys
    and bear the worn and weak.

In Christ nor black nor white,
    for God is color-blind;
all human hues the Lord invites
    to feasts of bread and wine.

In Christ nor straight nor gay,
    and we shall overcome
this final fear that blocks the day
    we dream of coming home.

In Christ we're neither nor,
    for all in Christ are one.
Sing praise to Christ the open door
    through whom all nations come!

Twelve Propositions on Same-Sex Relationships and the Church

1. Let it be said at once that the question of same-sex relationships and the church is a question of truth before it is a question of morality or discipline. Is the church's interpretation of scripture true? Is the church's traditional teaching true? If they are not, then they have to go, otherwise the faith of the church becomes *bad* faith. As Milton said, "Custom without truth is but agedness of error." One other thing in anticipation: Jesus said that the truth will make us free (John 8:32); Flannery O'-Connor added that "the truth will make you odd." But before we say anything more, we must know what we are saying it about. In most discussions on the issue of human sexuality we talk at each rather than with each other; in fact, we talk past each other.

2. I take it that homosexuality—and certainly the homosexuality I am talking about—is a given, not a chosen (not a "life-style choice"); a disposition recognised, not adopted; a condition as "normal" as left-handedness—or heterosexuality (whether by nature or nurture is a moot but morally irrelevant point). I also assume an understanding of human sexuality that is not over-genitalized, where friendship, intimacy, and joy are as important as libido, and where sexual acts themselves are symbolic as well as somatic. Needless to say, the "Yuk" factor deployed in some polemics has no place in rational discussion, while the language of "disease" and "cure" is ignorant and repugnant. Fundamentally, homosexuality is about who you are, not what you do, let alone what you get up to in bed. This is a descriptive point. There is also a normative point: I am talking about relationships that are responsible, loving, and faithful, not promiscuous, exploitative, or episodic.

3. What about the Bible? This is the Protestant question. "The Bible says," however, is a hopelessly inadequate and irrespon-

sible answer. Nevertheless, we must certainly examine specific texts — and then accept that they are universally condemnatory of homosexual practice. Arguments from silence — "Look at the relationship between David and Jonathan," or, "Observe that Jesus did not condemn the centurion's relationship with his servant" — are a sign of exegetical desperation. The Bible's unconditional No must simply be acknowledged. But No to *what*? For here is a fundamental hermeneutical axiom: "If Biblical texts on any social or moral topic are to be understood as God's word for us today, two conditions at least must be satisfied. There must be a resemblance between the ancient and modern social situation or institution or practice or attitude sufficient for us to be able to say that in some sense the text is talking about the same thing that we recognise today. And we must be able to demonstrate an underlying principle at work in the text which is consonant with biblical faith taken as a whole, and not contradicted by any subsequent experience or understanding."[1]

4. The first condition is not satisfied. The Bible knows nothing about homosexual orientation, or of homosexual relationships as defined in Proposition 2. In the Old Testament, the stories about Lot and his daughter (Genesis 19) and the Levite and his concubine (Judges 19) are about gang-bangs, while the prohibitions against homosexuality in the Holiness Code (Leviticus 18:22 and 20:13) are about (a) cultic cleanliness and (b) male dominance (i.e. a man should not treat another man like a woman). While purity concerns are not entirely anachronistic, Brueggemann is surely right to say that if push comes to shove, justice trumps purity.

5. More pertinent are attempts to ground an anthropology of heterosexuality in Genesis 1 and 2. But as sympathetic as I am to understanding the *imago Dei* in relational and social terms,

---

1. From a paper written by the Revd. Dr. Walter Houston, for circulation in the United Reformed Church, UK.

there are serious exegetical problems with this reading of Genesis 1:26–28, particularly if you read the text Christologically. As for Genesis 2, there is a rather obvious aetiological reason why a man and a woman would have to parent the human race, which says nothing about "compulsory" heterosexuality. There is certainly more to say about Adam and Eve than *not* Adam and Steve, and there is much in the rest of the Bible that would dissuade us from taking reproductive sex as the norm. Finally, a major omission from most references to the Old Testament: the Wisdom literature, with its emphasis on the observation of the world as a clue to discovering the way things are with God and creation, and therefore the suggestion that empiricism itself is biblical, and scientific findings germane to the discussion.

6. In the New Testament, the gospels are shtum about homosexuality. That leaves three references in the Pauline corpus (Jude 7 is irrelevant: cf. Genesis 19). The condemnations in I Corinthians 6:9–10 and I Timothy 1:8–11 depend on the translation of two obscure words (*malakoi* and *arsenokoitai*), but let us assume that they refer to same-sex relationships. There is certainly no question about the matter in Romans 1:18ff., undoubtedly the most relevant Pauline text about same-sex relationships. Or is there?

7. It is at least noteworthy that Paul deploys the language of dishonor and shame, rather than sin, to describe male-male relationships, which, in any case, are but a specific instance of the universal distortion of desire that enters the world as a result of the primal sin of idolatry. And Romans 1:26 is an interesting verse. We assume it refers to lesbianism (the only one in the Bible if it does), but the early Fathers, until John Chrysostom, and including Augustine, took it to refer to male-female anal intercourse. A cautionary tale here about the "obvious" meaning of a text! There is also the question of the rhetorical function of Romans 1:18ff.—or rather Romans 1:18–2:5. As James Alison observes (rightly ignoring conventional chapter and verse

divisions), Paul's argument works by condemning Gentile sexual practices — why? — so as to set his Jewish-Christian "hear-
ers up for a fall, and then delivering the coup de grace" (Romans
2:1), such that "the one use to which his reference could not be
put, without doing serious violence to the text, is a use which
legitimates any sort of judging"[2] such behavior.

8. More to the point, again, is the question of the nature of the
homosexual relationships being condemned. Are they the kind
of relationships defined in Proposition 2? Is, therefore, the first
condition of the hermeneutical axiom stated in Proposition 3
satisfied? The answer is No to both questions. The Hellenistic
homosexual relationships that Paul condemns, if not forms of
cultic prostitution, would normally have been both asymmet-
rical in terms of age, status, and power (the "approved" form
was pederasty) and therefore open to exploitation, as well as inherently transitory. And as Rowan Williams reflects on Romans 1: "Is it not a fair question to ask whether conscious
rebellion and indiscriminate rapacity could be presented as a
plausible account of the essence of 'homosexual behaviour', let
alone homosexual desire, as it may be observed around us
now,"[3] let alone in the church? Is the New Testament term
porneia an unequivocally accurate description?

9. Summing up the Old and New Testament texts as they con-
tribute to the contemporary discussion on homosexuality, the
late Gareth Moore says: "In so far as we can understand them,
they are not all concerned with the same things, they do not all
condemn the same things, and they do not all condemn what
they do for the same reasons. Most importantly, they do not

---

2. James Alison, *Underground God: Dispatches from the Scene of a Break-
In* (London: Continuum, 2006), pp. 137–38.

3. Rowan Williams, "Knowing Myself in Christ", in Timothy Brad-
shaw (ed.), *The Way Forward: Christian Voices on Homosexuality and the
Church* (London: Hodder & Stoughton, 1997), p. 16.

all condemn same-sex activity, some of them do not condemn same-sex activity, and *none of them* clearly condemns homosexual relationships or activity of a kind which is pertinent to the modern Christian debate."[4]

10. Unlike Protestants, Catholics approach the issue of same-sex relationships indirectly through the Bible but directly through tradition as interpreted by the magisterium. In particular, appeal is made to "natural law," norms of being and precepts for action said to be knowable apart from revelation, through ordinary experience and practical reason. Cultural pluralism and post-critical insights about the social construction of reality have radically problematized the concept of natural law. Nevertheless, the condemnation of same-sex relationships on the basis of natural law *even on its own terms* is intrinsically contingent. Thomas Aquinas himself accepted that natural law may not be immutable, and that specific judgements are open to change. With the Wisdom literature, empirical evidence is indispensable. One recalls Wittgenstein's advice: "Don't think, look!" And when one looks at gay and lesbian people, what does one see? Does one see defective heterosexuals with an inclination that is "objectively disordered" leading to behavior that is "intrinsically evil"? Whose experience? What evidence?

11. My own view is that, following the biblical trajectory (cf. the "underlying principle" in the second condition of the hermeneutical axiom stated in Proposition 3) of an ever-expanding inclusiveness of once marginalized people (Gentiles, women, blacks), it is only a question of time before the list expands to embrace homosexuals. Theologically, the issue before us is not that of "rights," or even justice or emancipation—the discourse of liberalism—it is a matter of divine grace and human and ecclesial ontology. The issues we have to tease out together in-

---

4. Gareth Moore, *A Question of Truth: Christianity and Homosexuality* (London: Continuum, 2003), p. 114.

clude biblical hermeneutics (particularly as it relates to the pre-
scriptive use of scripture in Christian ethics and to Augustine's
regula caritatis), empirical evidence, and personal experience.
With my own eyes I have seen the certainties, caricatures, and
phobias of Christians melt away through the warmth of contact and fellowship with lesbian and gay people, and, indeed—
crucially—through the visibility of their holiness and charisms.
The biblical paradigm is the story of the conversion of Cor-
nelius in Acts 10—which, of course, is actually the story of
the conversion of Peter himself, an "Aha!" moment before
"Truth's superb surprise" (Emily Dickinson)—an event which
sent the early church back to torah and tradition, trusting that
the Spirit would resolve its crisis, guide it into new heuristic
strategies of reading and interpretation, and lead it through a
risky and painful process of communal discernment to a kairotic
moment of decision.

12. For all Christians, as the drama unfolds, the question must
surely be this: How, as embodied and sexual creatures, do we
live in the truth of the gospel and witness to Christ? "Live in the
truth of the gospel": acting not according to law, either biblical or ecclesiastical, but not according to personal feelings either, rather following the truth that cannot but ultimately lead
to Christ, while refusing complicity in conspiracies of secrecy
and deceit, particularly in clerical culture. And "witness to
Christ": as forgiven sinners with no claims to infallibility, not
being judgmental on the one hand or contemptuous on the
other, and not seeking to score point against one's opponents,
or to back them into a corner, let alone bullying, un-church-
ing, even demonizing them. Amidst the rubble of cognitive
dissonance caused as the tectonic plates shift, the building
blocks of the future will be the practice of "hearing one another to speech" (Nelle Morton) and piles of patience and per-
severance, for (to conclude the Dickinson verse) "The Truth
must dazzle gradually/Or every man be blind." We will certainly discover what the church is made of, whether we Christians *really* trust the Spirit, practice peace, and live in hope.

Service

God's church is a school for learning

God's church is a school for learning,
    life-long learning in the Lord;
here we're taught to be discerning
    as we read and hear his Word.
Taught to dramatize the Story,
    Christians all have parts to play
in the theater of his glory,
    improvising on the way.

In the church of God are courses
    in the arts of peace and prayer,
and in using the resources
    from the files of love and care;
classes in the craft of living,
    seminars on grace and sin,
Sunday workshops in forgiving,
    coaching by the Christ within.

Thinking thoughts of God—what wonder!—
    trained in virtue, given space,
we will make mistakes and blunder,
    still in church there's always place:
place for all—here no exclusions—
    place for each—the fast and slow;
here we see through sight's illusions,
    here by faith alone we know.

Ten Propositions on Being a Theologian

1. Actually, there is no such thing as *a* theologian, anymore than there is such a thing as *a* Christian. Theologians are not solitary creatures. Theology is the outcome of good conversation, the conversation of friends. Though—the *rabies theologorum*—you could be forgiven for thinking the opposite! Which is why, in the interest of world peace, it is probably wise that theological conferences are held infrequently. Theologians are like horse manure: all in one place and they stink to high heaven; they are best spread around.

2. Theology is not free enterprise, and the theologian is not an entrepreneur. The theologian is a servant of the Word who, in communal conversation with other Christians, thinks about what God says to us in the Bible. Thus—but only thus—is she also a servant of the church, *creatura verbi Divini*. The theologian tests the church's preaching and teaching, and the work of other theologians, to keep them honest, i.e. to ensure that they are about the love and grace of God. A good theologian may be the bad conscience of the church.

3. The theologian, therefore, is not an academic but an ecclesiodemic. He may work *in* a university but he is not *of* the university. He must be multilingual, but he must remember that his hometown is Jerusalem, not Athens. So he must hang loose to criteria of academic respectability. Submission, for example, to the idea that theology must never be homiletical, or that a theologian should not begin a lecture with prayer, suggests a Babylonian captivity. To switch biblical geography, the theologian must not hanker after the fleshpots of Nile College.

4. Can a theologian be an unbeliever? Don't be ridiculous! Theology is *fides quaerens intellectum*: no *fides*, no *intellectum*. And while anyone may interpret the Bible, only a believer interprets the Bible *as scripture*. Moreover, one can speak *about* God only as one speaks *to* God. Prayer is the epistemological precondition of theology, which to issue in *pietas* must begin with in-

vocation. *Lex orandi, lex credendi, lex agendi.* A prayerless theologian is an oxymoron; indeed a prayerless theologian is a
moron—which is not to say that God cannot use the braying
of Balaam's ass.

5. Since the twelfth century the notion has been around that the
theologian is a speculator in ideas, and since the Enlightenment that he is a specialist in certain distinct areas of enquiry.
We must lament the eclipse of the holistic theologian, the theologian who is also a mystic, and insist that theologians can
responsibly teach the faith only as they live a holy life. And the
notion that the specialized theologian can be biblical, historical, dogmatic, or pastoral without all these disciplines
encroaching on each other is a cloven fiction indeed.

6. Theology (with Aquinas, Calvin, Barth) is thus a very spiritual matter, and a very practical, very ethical matter. In fact
the theologian, as a student of the humanity of God, is the
quintessential humanist. She will have in her sights not only
God but also the good, God in his perfections and humanity
in its perfectibility, i.e. she will be concerned with human flour-
ishing. And as humans can flourish only in community—in
the *polis*—a question that one should always ask about a theologian is: How does her theology politic?

7. All good theology is always contextual theology. Which is not
to say that the context sets the agenda of the theologian, because
contexts never come neat, they are not self-interpreting. It is
to say that the theologian works at the interface of text and
context, and seeks to address specific text to specific context.
And contexts change. By isolating and repeating texts apart
from their own contemporary contexts, theologians are not
faithful; on the contrary, they inevitably betray the faith by
anachronism. The letters of Paul—all occasional, none systematic—and particularly the apostle's imaginative engagement with scripture—are the paradigm for the theologian.

8. The theologian will be a person who, off his knees, can think
on his feet, "Thinking incessantly," as Elizabeth Jennings

describes the Angelic Doctor in her poem "Thomas Aquinas," "making cogitations always but as keenly,/freshly as the child/He had been who asked repeatedly 'What is God?'" You have heard of astronauts: a theologian is a "theonaut." He will also be a *bricoleur*, who retrieves and selects his materials eclectically, and recalibrates them tactically. If the Holy Spirit is a dove, the theologian is a cuckoo, free to squat in any nest—and steal the eggs. Incorrigibly kleptomaniacal, while the theologian may not long for Egypt, he may certainly rip off the Egyptians.

9. The bottom line of all theological endeavor is the practical, performative life of the local church. Strictly speaking, all believers are theologians, because all believers, willy-nilly, think about God. The only question is whether we think well or poorly. It is not the theologian's job to think about God for us, it is the theologian's job to help us think about God better, so that we may believe, pray, serve, live, and die better. Dorothy Sayers said that "Christians would rather die than think—and most of them do." The theologian is out to make Ms. Sayers a liar.

10. Ultimately, of course, theologians do not know what they are talking about. So they should exercise meticulous word-care—and not talk too much. I often think that books of theology should contain occasional blank pages, to signal the reader to pause, in silence and wonder. There will be no theology in the eschaton. Before the divine *doxa*, we will confess, with St. Thomas, "All my work is like straw." Karl Barth famously said that when he gets to heaven he will seek out Mozart before Calvin. Quite right—and presumably he spoke to Calvin only to compare errors. Me—I'll be heading for the choir of angels, to find Sandy Koufax (if, that is, he precedes me!), to see how he made the baseball sing.

We look for God in nature's world

We look for God in nature's world,
    for nature's world is from God's hand;
on earth expecting heav'n unfurled,
    we scan the sky, the sea, the land:
but though we search with eye and mind,
the God we seek we cannot find.

We look for God in works of art,
    for works of art the Lord inspires;
speaking to human soul and heart,
    sparking a deep divine desire:
but though we search with eye and mind,
the God we seek we cannot find.

We look for God in moral sense,
    for moral sense the Lord instills;
in right and wrong the evidence
    for the Lawgiver's sovereign will:
but though we search with eye and mind,
the God we seek we cannot find.

God looks for us in God's own Son,
    in Jesus Christ, and Christ alone;
and at the cross the search is done,
    the lost are found and carried home:
our search for God? — we're blind as bats! —
like mice gone looking for a cat.

So look for God in God's own Son,
    in Jesus Christ, and Christ alone;
no enterprise beneath the sun,
    nor any human knowledge known,
can ever show what God, by grace,
reveals to us in Jesus' face.

Ten Propositions on Karl Barth: Theologian

1. Karl Barth was a *Reformed* theologian. Sounds like a no-brainer. And, yes, fundamental motifs of Barth's theology have a definite Reformed pedigree—the glory, majesty, and grace of God; the primacy of the Word in Holy Scripture; the polemic against idolatry; the doctrine of election; the relationship between gospel and law; sanctification. But for Barth, the Reformed tradition was not so much a body of doctrine as a habit of mind. Observe that Barth got himself up to speed with Reformed dogmatics only after he had become famous for his two editions of *The Epistle to the Romans* and taken up a lectureship at Göttingen. His was a *theologia reformata* only as it was also a *theologia semper reformanda*. His conversations with his Reformed forefathers, while deferential, were always critical. And the doctrines he inherited he always re-worked with daring and imagination.

2. Karl Barth was an *ecumenical* theologian. While recognising that theology is always confessional—there is no Archimedean point, you've got to stand and start somewhere—Barth insisted that the *intentio theologiae* must be catholic. His net was broad, its mesh tight, and he cast it far and wide: the magisterial Reformers, of course, but also the Fathers West and East, the medieval schoolmen, the Protestant scholastics, the nineteenth-century liberals. Barth had a vibrant belief in the *communio sanctorum*, and could echo Faulkner: "The past is not dead. It is not even past." The universal church was Barth's oyster, and he found pearls (as well as grit!) throughout its history. His Catholic colleague at Basel, Hans Urs von Balthasar, paid Barth the ultimate compliment when he said that his friend was "a theologian and not a reformer."

3. Karl Barth was an *ecclesial* theologian. When Barth began his writing and teaching career, theology was in captivity to the university. His teacher Adolf Harnack was aghast at his student's cavalier attitude to the academically respectable histor-

ical-critical method, and his liberal peers dismayed by their colleague's hostility to apologetics. However, for Barth theology is the servant of the church, which conforms to the syllabus of Jerusalem, not Athens, and checks its performances not against reason or experience but against the authoritative script of Scripture. Hence Barth's mature theology settled into the form of *Church Dogmatics*. The German title is *Die kirchliche Dogmatik*, which (George Hunsinger observes) might just as accurately be rendered *Ecclesial Theology*. And as the heart of the church is worship, so the soul of theology is prayer. For Barth, we can talk *about* God only because and as we talk *to* God.

4. Karl Barth was an *exegetical* theologian. Barth's theology began in preaching; it is a homiletical theology. Interpreters of Barth who have not toiled in the study preparing sermons and trembled in the pulpit preaching them are at a distinct, if not fatal, disadvantage. And while Barth said that "preaching is exposition, not exegesis," it certainly begins in exegesis, which he understood as the prayerful attentiveness to "the strange new world of the Bible." Although Barth moved from the pulpit to the lectern and preached very little until the end of his career, exegesis always lay at the heart of his dogmatic enterprise. It is not surprising, therefore, that some readers of the *Church Dogmatics* skip the large print altogether and go for the fine print of Barth's close yet creative readings of scripture. Barth would be horrified at the widespread biblical illiteracy in today's church, and were he suddenly to appear in our midst, his first words to us would no doubt be the same as his last words to his students at Bonn before he departed for Basel in 1935: "Exegesis, exegesis, and yet more exegesis!"

5. Karl Barth was a *moral* theologian. For Barth, the imperative of ethics is inextricably connected to the indicative of dogmatics. In announcing who he is, God tells us what to do. But for Barth the moral life is not rule-based, nor even biblicist: dogmatically mediated and contextually located, it is, above all, a matter of prayerful and thoughtful discernment. Nor is

obedience a burden, indeed it is perfect *freedom*: it is law precisely as gospel. And it begins in gratitude: "Grace," Barth said, "evokes gratitude like the voice of an echo. Gratitude follows grace like thunder lightning." Barth would have agreed with Blake: "The thankful receiver bears a plentiful harvest." He would also have had some sympathy with Blake's radical politics! For Barth there was no such thing as a purely personal ethics; as a moral theologian he was, ipso facto, a *political* theologian. The author of the Barmen Declaration declared: "A silent community, merely observing the events of the time, would not be a Christian community." And while the "Red pastor" of Safenwil knew that the left often gets it wrong, he mischievously suggested that conservatives rarely get it right.

6. Karl Barth was a *scientific* theologian. Not that Barth engaged with the natural sciences. Indeed his disciple Thomas Torrance found Barth's indifference to science, and his conviction that science and theology are not only non-interactive but non-complementary disciplines, to be perhaps the greatest weakness of his mentor. Nor was Barth the least bit interested in methodology, or in hermeneutics as a theoretical question. Rather Barth was scientific in the sense of the German *wissenschaftlich*: he tailored his theology to fit the nature of the object of its investigation, namely the person and work of God. Perhaps counter-intuitively, Barth's theology was strictly scientific precisely because it was so exactingly trinitarian and Christological.

7. Karl Barth was a *poetic* theologian. Indeed Maurice Wiles described Barth as a "theological poet." Not since Luther has a theologian used such colloquial, energetic, and expressive language. Formally, Barth rejected rhetoric — "No eloquence!" was a slogan of his, particularly in preaching; materially, he was a master of it. Indeed Stephen H. Webb devotes a whole book to the subject: *Re-Figuring Theology: The Rhetoric of Karl Barth* (1991). And quite right, because how you say something is a significant part of the something you say. And because he

was speaking about *God*, how could Barth avoid stretching his God-*talk* to breaking point—dialectical discourse corresponding to a dynamic deity, the word on the wing imitating (as he put it) "a bird in flight"? Barth is particularly adept in his deployment of irony and hyperbole, and his metaphors are always apt, memorable, and often explosive, a quality that attracted the novelist John Updike. Hence too Flannery O'Connor's bon mot: "I like old Barth. He throws the furniture around."

8. Karl Barth was a *contextual* theologian. In *Karl Barth: Against Hegemony* (1999), Timothy Gorringe demonstrates how Barth's theology interfaces with and responds to the events of his time, how socially situated it is—even if often "against the stream." In a sense, all Barth's work is occasional. In June 1933, when he said that the urgent task was to get on with theology "as if nothing has happened," he was not suggesting that the church withdraw to the hills in denial of the Nazification of Germany, rather he was declaring that National Socialism must not be allowed to set the agenda for the church. For Barth, theology must be related to the contemporary without being dominated by the contemporary, and so "more like the needle of a compass than a weather vane" (Eberhard Busch). Barth himself said: "My thinking, writing, and speaking developed from reacting to people, events, and circumstances with which I was involved." But Barth also said: "Revelation is not a predicate of history, but history is a predicate of revelation." So, yes, the Bible in one hand—the right hand; the newspaper in the other—the left.

9. Karl Barth was a *joyful* theologian. The evangel was at the center of his life as well as his thought. But he delighted in the truth wherever he found it: bilingual, Barth was equally fluent in the languages of Zion and Babylon. Like God himself, he was an unashamed humanist, and an irrepressible lover of God's good creation. Of course he adored Mozart, but, a keen filmgoer, he was also head-over-heels about Marlene Dietrich, whom he intended to give a place in *Church Dogmatics*, "prob-

ably in eschatology." And *hilaritas*, for Barth, was an inestimable virtue. "What a pity," he once said about some over-earnest fundamentalists, that they don't "think it worth mentioning that human beings are the only creatures that laugh." And one of his grandchildren wondered whether "the many creases in my face had developed because I spent so much of my life laughing." And laughing at himself too. Just four days before he died in 1968, aged 82, Barth told some friends that he had finally found out why there was no end to his volumes of *Dogmatics*—"the lady in the hoop skirt," all 28.6 pounds of her: "My doctors discovered that my colon was much too long." No wonder Barth has been called the "happiest theologian of our age."

10. Karl Barth was a *nomadic* theologian. He was always a pilgrim *in via*, writing his doxological *Dogmatics* in a tent rather than a temple. It sounds trite to say that Barth was a theologian for all the ages, but it is surely significant that he has been called a modern, late modern, and post-modern thinker, with, for example, some scholars pointing to the obvious influence of Kant and Hegel, while others draw parallels with Wittgenstein and Derrida. The *Church Dogmatics*, of course, remained incomplete, an unfinished symphony, an un-spired cathedral. But perhaps that is not so much because Barth ran out of time, perhaps it is because *any* dogmatics is inherently a work in progress, a fragment however huge. After all, every end is, in fact, a new beginning; it is just that we seldom recognize it at the time.

The church of God is always slow

The church of God is always slow
    to follow where the Spirit leads;
a pilgrim people on the go,
    yet hesitant to move at speed.

We meet in councils and debate,
    we keep the church in good repair,
we manage and administrate,
    but have no time to dream and dare.

We sit in buildings all aloof,
    remembering the days of yore;
we're more concerned about the roof
    than hunger, justice, peace, and war.

And why begrudge the Spirit's work
    outside the church, among the throng?
Or is it only Christian folk
    who speak the truth and right the wrong?

Confess, the church is out of touch,
    we're all at sea, becalmed, marooned.
Repent, for God is not a crutch,
    and not a bandage but the wound.

O Holy Spirit, burn and blow,
    and drive us on, full steam ahead;
no turning back, no contraflow,
    but constant rising from the dead.

Ten Propositions on Being a Minister

A few years ago, as part of a working group in the Welsh Synod of the United Reformed Church in the United Kingdom, I wrote a report to launch a program for local churches to explore the question "What are ministers for?" It was entitled *Great Expectations*. I began by deconstructing the question, suggesting that its pragmatism (as I would now put it) is theologically vulgar, and that, in any case, it begs a couple of questions: namely, that before we can say what *ministers* are for, we need to know what the *church* is for; and before we can say what the church is for, we need to know what *God* is up to. And as what God is up to is nothing less than cosmic reconciliation and renewal, and as the church is called to bear witness to God's great work-in-progress, insofar as ministers are "for" anything, it has to do with helping to align the church with the *missio Dei*.

Having thrown a spanner into the works, I then got down to some nuts and bolts. Here is an adapted summary.

1. Ministers should be able to lead and to organize, but they are not called to be managers. And woe unto the minister who would run the one, holy, catholic, apostolic—and "efficient"—McChurch!

2. Ministers should be able to conduct worship winsomely and to preach intelligently. But woe unto the minister who would be an entertainer or cheerleader—or turn prayer into a "resource."

3. Ministers should be able to listen, empathize, care, counsel, and give spiritual direction—i.e. help people discern the word of God in their lives—but they are not called to be therapists, let alone life-style coaches. And woe unto the minister who would turn out well-balanced citizens who make the system work!

4. Ministers are not called to be casual visitors, but they should certainly be sharing in the lives of their people, and meeting them where they are most truly themselves, in the quotidian as well as the crisis—often at home and, for chaplaincies, at

work—laughing with those who laugh and weeping with those who weep.

5. Ministers are not called to be scholars, but they need to rediscover their roles as community theologians (as teachers, not just "facilitators"). Breaking "the strange silence of the Bible in the church" (James Smart), they must ensure that the scriptures are at the center of congregational life, and that, at a time of epidemic "Theological Deficit Disorder," their churches are cultures of learning. They must also ensure that the hermeneutical and ethical tasks are one, shaping character as well as transforming minds.

6. Ministers are not called to be scientists or sociologists, but they should be keen observers of, and articulate commentators on, what is happening in the world, to enable their congregations to engage their faith with their life and work, vigilantly discern the signs of the times, and boldly witness to Christ in the *polis*.

7. Ministers are not chairmen of the board, and their ministries should be exercised collaboratively. And ministers should not be doing what others can do, otherwise they disempower them and rob them of their own ministries. Making themselves as redundant and unnecessary as possible, ministers should help people to discover and deploy their own particular grace-gifts, equipping the saints for building up the body of Christ.

8. Ministers are shepherds—though many a congregant would prefer a pet lamb. As they call their flock to new pastures, and to experimental patterns and models of ministry, they are inevitably going to irritate and unsettle some of the fat sheep. So ministers must expect to be butted. Another zoological metaphor: ministers should be horseflies, not butterflies— better to be swatted than mounted.

9. Ministers represent the local church to the wider church, and the wider church to the local church—and the church is very wide. You know the story of the Welsh *parch* who was finally rescued after years stranded on a desert island, where he had

built a little village: when the sailors asked why he had constructed *two* churches, he replied, "*That* is the one I *don't* attend." Ministers should nurture ecumenical collegiality. And if it is said that an ecumenical freeze has set in, remember Emily Dickinson's couplet: "Winter under cultivation/Is as arable as spring."

10. Finally, ministers, remember this: your congregations are unlikely to resemble the early church in Acts, so whenever you get stressed out, read Paul's Corinthian correspondence—and thank God for the awkward folk he has given *you* to love!

Let us listen for the Word

Let us listen for the Word,
as we hear it read and preached,
sharper than the sharpest sword,
sweeter than the sweetest peach.

Scripture sings in different keys—
hymns of praise and mournful cries,
letters, legends, histories,
guidance from the worldly-wise.

Written with imperfect scores,
pitched for people culture-bound,
scarred by old barbaric laws—
scripture makes discordant sounds.

Yet a love-song, with refrain,
resonates from all around;
sunshine breaks through cloud and rain,
flowers bloom from barren ground.

God whose Word is cruciform,
as we hear it preached and read,
may our hearts be strangely warmed,
and our souls raised from the dead.

Ten Propositions on Preaching

1. What is a sermon? Wrong question. A sermon is not a what but a who. A sermon is Jesus Christ expectorate. You eat the book; it is sweet in the mouth but bitter in the stomach (Revelation 10:9–11); you spit out the Word and spray the congregation. When grace hits the mark, it always begins with an unpleasant recoil. Luther said the word of God confronts us as *adversarius noster*.

2. A sermon starts in silence. First silence before the impossible: Who can speak the word of *God*? Then the silence of expectation: God has *called* you to preach—and God is faithful. Before a preacher preaches, she must *not* preach, she must *listen*; and when she *does* preach, it is only because she *has* to preach. God gave us one mouth and two ears—and the preacher must use them in that proportion.

3. Sermon preparation is primarily the preparation of the preacher, not the preached. The preparation of the sermon itself will only be as rigorous as the *askesis* (spiritual regime) of the preacher. Pray for the presence of the Holy Spirit—and then work like stink. If the Holy Spirit hasn't been with the preacher in the study, he's not going to accompany the lazy so-and-so into the pulpit. A tip: watch out for texts that "pinch": they're probably trying to tell you something. A must: sermons should be written: that'll ensure that you actually hear what you're saying.

4. Context, context, context. A text without a context is a pretext. The context of scripture, of course, but also the contemporary context—the Bible in one hand, the broadsheet in the other. The clash of two worlds: *scriptura probat mundum*. And there is the local context: the community in which you live, its people, their stories, yourself. But be careful: the sermon must interpret the contemporary context, not the other way round. The context is the setting of the sermon, but it must not call the shots.

5. Relevance? Blow relevance! It is God who determines the nature of relevance. Who wants to hear about relevance? For example, the forgiveness of sins, the whole of the gospel, is relevant — not because, as the world thinks, the forgiver finds inner healing, but because the guilty one is a sufferer in need of acceptance and embrace. When relevance rules, the tail of the world wags the dog of the church. In *Moby-Dick* Herman Melville likens the world to "a ship on its passage out, ... and the pulpit is its prow," its "foremost part; all the rest comes in its rear; the pulpit leads the world."

6. The gospel itself is not "repent and be forgiven" — that is sheer legalism — but "you are forgiven — and *therefore* now *free* to repent." Even pagans say, "If you're sorry, I'll forgive you." More to the evangelical point, how can we repent of sin when sin is known only as sin forgiven, when we can know ourselves as sinners only in the light of grace?

7. Technique? Skills? Voice coaching? Forget about them. A sermon is not oratory, a sermon is *sui generis*. Besides, all theological speech is broken speech. Moses had a stammer, and Paul was embarrassingly ineloquent. Smooth tongues are often forked. What has been called "word-care," however, particularly in an age of frivolous and mendacious loquacity, is a different matter: the practice of word-care is crucial. Literature — particularly poetry — is the school of word-care. Remember: you are responsible for every word you preach.

8. And the latest technology? Woe unto "techies"! Technically, Richard Lischer observes "that when the brain is asked to multitask by listening and watching at the same time, it always quits listening."[1] Substantively, if the medium is the message, how can the medium of IT — the machine of postmodern power and

---

1. Richard Lischer, *The End of the World: The Language of Reconciliation in a Culture of Violence* (Grand Rapids, Michigan: William B. Eerdmans, 2005), p.25.

depthless image—square with the vulnerable and iconoclastic word of the cross? Lischer provides a thought-experiment: "What would Martin Luther King's 'I Have a Dream' speech look like in PowerPoint?"[2] Or think of Charlton Heston playing Moses in the film *The Ten Bullet Points*. Technology: "the knack of so arranging the world that we don't have to experience it" (Max Frisch).

9. Your congregation—know it, live it, love it. This is the *koinonia* of preacher and community, and it must lie at the heart of every sermon. If you don't laugh and weep with your people, you've got no right to expect them to hear you preach. And don't be afraid to have specific individuals in the congregation in mind when you preach: we reach the universal through the particular.

10. Finally, preach like there is no tomorrow—because there isn't: in the sermon tomorrow is already today. Homiletics is eschatology. On the other hand, if you haven't struck oil within twenty minutes, stop boring!

---

2. Ibid., p. 26.

Scripture is a conversation

Scripture is a conversation,
Ezra, Jonah, Peter, Paul;
hidden is God's revelation,
told to some but meant for all.

Like a conference, many speakers
vie to make their voices heard;
only to the eyes of seekers
is disclosed the living Word.

We are called to be discerning
as we eavesdrop on the text;
not for answers but for learning
may the Spirit richly vex.

Move me from my fixed opinions,
axe laid to the frozen sea;
Lord, I long for your dominion,
liberated from my "me".

Thus unthreatened by the other,
unconcerned with being wrong,
may we add with sister, brother,
to your all-inclusive song.

9.5 Theses on Listening to Preaching

1. *Preparing.* You *must* prepare because you *may* prepare. God is about to gift you with the gospel! Although you cannot do anything to *be* ready for it, you must do everything you can to *get* ready for it. You rightly expect the preacher to prepare before he preaches—and he rightly expects *you* to prepare before you listen. No lazy so-and-sos in the pulpit or the pew!

2. *Expecting.* When the preacher speaks, God will speak—to *you*: that must be not only your hope but also your expectation. So what that the Revd. Bloggs is errant and inept? The power of the sermon no more depends on the excellence of the preacher than the effectiveness of the eucharist depends on the character of the president. Treasure comes in cracked clay jars. Homiletics too is *theologia crucis*.

3. *Focusing.* More precisely, *attendre*, which is a "waiting" as well as a "centering." This is never easy, but in contemporary culture, where the word has been displaced by the image and most people have the attention span of a gnat, it is harder than ever. Assume the same posture for the sermon as you do for prayer: resolute yet relaxed. Then fasten your seatbelt. (All churches should come equipped with seatbelts.)

4. *Discerning.* There is, of course, no guarantee that God will speak to you through the preacher. The preacher may come with gold —or with fool's gold. You must test the spirits—which means that you must be *critical*. You must listen not only *to* the Word but also *for* the Word—which means (as the Reformers taught) that you must distinguish between *Bible* and *gospel*.

5. *Praying.* Critical intelligence is a necessary condition for listening to the sermon, but it is not a sufficient condition for hearing the gospel. Only the Holy Spirit can give us the ears of evangelical faith and understanding. *Veni, Creator Spiritus!* *Epiclesis* is as crucial in the ministry of the Word as it is in the ministry of the sacrament.

6. *Dying.* "When Christ calls us, he bids us come and die" (Bonhoeffer). Every act of worship is a funeral. In the sermon the preacher hereby notifies the congregation that it is dead and buried—an ex-people. This is not a metaphor, this is our reality *coram Deo*. Listen to the sermon as if it were your own obituary—it is. Judgement is *now*.

7. *Rising.* The sermon is your own obituary—it is also the announcement of your own re-birth. The preacher has been likened to a surgeon; she is also a midwife. If the first reaction to the sermon is recoil, the ultimate response is "Rejoice!"— and pass around the cigars! The non-people are a new people! Resurrection is *now*.

8. *Serving.* One who hears the Word but does not do the Word has not heard the Word. George Herbert said that "sermons are dangerous things; that none goes out of church as he came in." "Pastor," said the worshipper, "what a wonderful sermon!" "That," replied the preacher, "remains to be seen." When the liturgy is over, the *leitourgia* (service in the world) begins: your ministry of reconciliation and liberation.

9. *Persevering.* Once you belong to a church, the only grounds for leaving it are heresy or apostasy. Lousy preaching, alas, is not a *status confessionis*. Besides, God does not speak only from the pulpit, he speaks in the readings, prayers, creeds, and communion. Bear with your preacher—he may be a cross sent for you to bear!—and make him a better preacher by being a better listener ...

9.5 ... though *heckling* might help too!

God, in many ways you meet us

God, in many ways you meet us,
    speak to us in world and church,
in the quake and in the quiet,
    when we flee and as we search.

In the splendor of the sunlight,
    in the sparkle of a star,
we see something of your glory,
    catch a glimpse of who you are.

On the canvas of an artist,
    in composer's sacred song,
through the verse and voice of poet,
    we sense worlds for which we long.

In the otherness of stranger
    and familiar face of friend,
we are entertaining angels
    whom your holy love commends.

When our lives are running smoothly,
    when our hopes have turned to dust,
through our joys and through our sorrows,
    in your providence we trust.

God, in word and wine we meet you
    in this sacramental space;
from the pulpit, on the table,
    close encounters with your grace.

Ten Propositions on the Literal and the Literary

1. The more *literal*, the less *literary* a person is likely to be—and vice-versa. A survey of the reading habits of fundamentalists would be an interesting exercise. I suspect that they would score low on reading classical and Booker/Pulitzer prize fiction—and even lower on poetry. I wonder what they would make of William Empson's seminal study *Seven Types of Ambiguity*? To plagiarize Paul, the literal crucifies, the literary resurrects: meaning walks through closed doors. "Tell all the Truth but tell it slant" (Emily Dickinson).

2. It is an interesting fact that fundamentalism is predominantly a Protestant phenomenon, a *reductio ad absurdum* of the Reformers' emphasis on the literal meaning of scripture to the exclusion the medieval "fourfold vision" (Blake). Is there a lurking fear here of a connection between polyvalence and polytheism? How ironic that, on the contrary, an insistence on a single, solid, certain meaning—i.e. semantic closure—is indicative of idolatry. The burning bush is the horticulture of divine deconstruction, and the golden calf is bull.

3. Another interesting fact: the rise of Protestant literalism went hand in hand with the desacralization of nature, which—the good news—entailed the rise of the natural sciences, but which also—the bad news—issued in the evacuation of God from the material world, soon followed by the absence of God from the world of culture. Modernist atheism itself is the spawn of biblical literalism. And when belief did a bunk, it was the priesthood of poets that helped keep the rumor of transcendence alive. In *Real Presences*, George Steiner argues that "everything we recognize as being of compelling stature in literature … is of a religious inspiration or reference," and

that the act of reading … is a metaphysical and, in the last analysis, a theological one."[1]

4. So another connection: the "disenchantment" of nature (Weber) and the impoverishment of the imagination. Chesterton observed a "combination between logical completeness and spiritual contraction." And he said: "Poetry is sane because it floats easily in an infinite sea; reason seeks to cross the infinite sea, and so makes it finite."[2] There is also the spiritual contraction, the failure of imagination, of legalism and moralism. Hence R.S. Thomas' description of Welsh Nonconformity as "the adroit castrator/Of art".[3]

5. There is much discussion about whether or not theology is a science. Karl Barth insisted that it is. But Barth himself was a master of stirring rhetoric and stunning imagery. And, of course, there was his passion for Mozart, and his admiration for Dostoevsky's *The Brothers Karamazov* and Melville's *Moby-Dick*. Barth wasn't so hot on the visual arts—his Protestant prejudice showing—but the *Church Dogmatics* is a magnificent cathedral, stained glass windows and all. In short, if theology is a science, it is also an art.

6. Which should not be the least bit surprising. After all, God-talk is impossible without the deployment of analogy and metaphor, and the Bible is incomprehensible apart from a narrative hermeneutics. Is it therefore not a scandal that, until recent times, theology has been in thrall to an ontological and epistemological captivity—and inevitable that it would take a Catholic, Hans Urs von Balthasar, to remind us of the *beauty* of God and to write a theological aesthetics and dramatics? Is

---

1. George Steiner, *Real Presences* (Chicago: University of Chicago Press, 1991), pp. 215–16.

2. G.K. Chesterton, *Orthodoxy* (London: Hodder & Stoughton, 1996 [first published in 1908]), pp. 18, 14.

3. R.S. Thomas, "The Minister", in *Selected Poems: 1946–1968* (London: Granada, 1983 [first published in 1973]), p. 31.

not grace graceful? Is not faith itself an imaginative perception of reality?

7. Theological ethics—another test case. Fundamentalist ethics are rule-based, and the answers to moral problems are found, decontextualised, at the back of the (good) book. Jesus' preferred method of ethical instruction, however, is the parable, "subversive speech" (William R. Herzog II). Indeed in *The Moral Vision of the New Testament* (1996), Richard B. Hays argues that a "*symbolic world* as context for moral discernment" is fundamental to the Bible. "The kingdom of God is like this." Enter the story, work it out—then *act* it out.

8. Follow the trajectory to *virtue ethics*. The accent is on agency and action, dispositions and desire, time and telos. Rules are not excluded, but they function heuristically, as "perspicuous descriptive summaries of good judgments" (Martha Nussbaum), to inculcate habits appropriate to the development of Christ-like character. Moral theology works best when it tells the stories of the saints. Virtue ethics is narrative ethics, where the script is unfinished and improvisation is essential. The Christian life is jazz.

9. One of the great filmic send-ups of biblical literalism: the opening scene of Monty Python's *Life of Brian*. The camera pans to Jesus preaching the Sermon on the Mount, and then to a group at a distance where our Lord's voice doesn't quite carry. "Blessed are the cheese makers," one character hears. "What's so special about the cheese makers?" asks a woman. "Obviously it is not to be taken literally," her husband replies; "it refers to any manufacturer of dairy products."

10. Moral: a cultureless theology is an ecclesiastical disaster—and a "two culture" (C.P. Snow) theology is not much better. If we are ignorant of science we get top marks in "Stupidity 101: Creationism." But if we are ignorant of literature, the merely ignorant becomes downright dangerous—witness the nonsensical interpretations of biblical apocalyptic by the Religious Right and its pernicious influence on American foreign policy in the

Middle East. If pastors should be community theologians, community theologians should be writers-in-residence, exercising what John Howard Yoder called "word-care," and teaching their congregations how to *read*.

Slavery

Lord, behold a wretched sinner

Lord, behold a wretched sinner,
from the outer to the inner;
at repentance, rank beginner:
    day and night my conscience cries.

Where begin? My faults keep mounting;
when I start I can't stop counting;
huge the sum, but Christ's accounting
    crosses out and nullifies.

Good I would but can't achieve it,
bad I hate but can't relieve it.
God for us? I can't believe it:
    me the apple of his eye!

God forgives before petition;
grace alone shows our condition;
truth demands our self-suspicion:
    like a snake the heart is sly.

While accusing scribes are hissing,
Christ portrays the Father kissing
cheek of child that he's been missing:
    Love forgives and sanctifies!

Ten Propositions on Sin

What is the nature of our sin
That it deserves so beautifully
To be forgiven?
—R. S. Thomas

1. Reinhold Niebuhr famously described original sin as the one
   empirically verifiable Christian doctrine. Niebuhr was wrong.
   We know where his statement's purchase comes from: the omnipresent reality of self-alienation and social disorder. But sin
   is a theologoumenon, and, like all theologoumena, it is a matter of faith, not of disinterested observation. To be specific, sin
   is a matter of faith because, definitively, it is a disruption between human beings and God—and the knowledge of God is
   itself a matter of faith. In fact, it takes grace to bring to light
   the true nature—and darkness—of sin.

2. What is the nature of this disruption? The fundamental form of
   sin is *disobedience*. "The Lord God commanded …" (Genesis
   2:16)—and our paradisal parents did not do as they were told.
   They transgressed the "Thou shalt not," they trespassed on the
   Edenic orchard. As Paul typologically interprets Genesis 3 in
   Romans 6, the key terms are Adam's *parabasis* and *parakoe* (disobedience) and, in contrast, Christ's *hupakoe* (obedience). It is
   precisely as the obedient one that Jesus is the sinless one, and
   precisely as the sinless one that he is *peccator pessimus* (Luther),
   the worst of sinners, the one who accepts the sin we refuse to
   acknowledge. The heart of sin is its denial, the self-deceit of innocence—and its projection on others, our scapegoats.

3. Do I take the story of the "fall" in Genesis 3 to be "history"? No
   more than I take the three-story universe of Genesis 1 to be "science." So the story of the fall isn't true? Don't be silly! Only a
   discredited positivism would reduce truth to the "facts" of history and science. Robert Jenson, however, does take Adam and
   Eve to be actual hominids, "the first community of our bio-

logical ancestors who disobeyed God's command."[1] Jenson's target is an idealist understanding of the fall as a "myth," but his
paleo-anthropological alternative is, in my view, a category mistake. The fall is neither a timeless idea nor a chronological moment but a pre-historical narrative disclosure of the way it is
with you and me. The fall is a foil to the history of humanity.

4. The fall-as-foil forestalls two other errors. First, "The Bible
knows no 'sinless man' and consequently no state of innocence";[2] thus the fall "is not a fall in the sense that man after has
become anything else than man was before."[3] And, second, the
story of the fall is not an aetiological narrative; it is not an explanation of sin. There *is* no explanation of sin. Sin is sure—
and sin is a surd: irrational, non-necessary, non-sensical.
Kierkegaard, that great anatomist of sin, is our teacher here.

5. After disobedience, there are several contenders for the dia-
bolical crown of foundational sin. Pride of place in the history of harmatology goes to—*pride*; Reinhold Niebuhr perhaps
gives the definitive modern account. Feminist theologians have
objected that this tradition, culturally androcentric, actually
colludes in the oppression of women, abetting self-hatred and
docility at the expense of self-respect and empowerment. Liberation theologians argue the same case with respect to color
and class. The point should be acknowledged. However rather
than abandon the tradition, I think it would be wiser to re-
configure our understanding of pride—and to supplement
it. Taking faith as *fiducia*, Richard Niebuhr focuses on its opposite, *mistrust*. Karl Barth, theologian of grace, appropri-
ately accents *ingratitude*. In Thomas Mann's retelling of the
Faust legend, *Doctor Faustus*, the satanic counter-command-
ment is "Thou shalt not love," a motif central to Schleierma-

1. Robert Jenson, *Systematic Theology, Volume II* (New York: Oxford University Press, 1999), p. 150.
2. Claus Westermann, *Creation* (London: SCM Press, 1971), p. 110.
3. Bruce Vawter, *On Genesis: A New Reading* (London: Geoffrey Chap-
man, 1977), p. 79.

cher and common in liberal theology. And to add to the witches' brew, consider Augustine's take on sin as *concupiscentia*, disordered desire, a particularly apt category for evaluating our obsessionally consumerist society. However, Luther's graphic image of the sinner as *homo incurvatus in se* is perhaps the paradigm of sin that best combines incisiveness with comprehensiveness.

6. A word on "total depravity." Calvin's doctrine develops Augustine and Luther's insight that we are, in Alistair McFadyen's double-entendre, "bound to sin."[4] It is both polemical and dogmatic. Polemically, it is an attack on Origen's platonic privileging of the mind, and Erasmus' privileging of the will, over against the "lower appetites." Thus does Calvin correctly interpret the Pauline category of *sarx*. Dogmatically, total depravity means not that human beings are vile and loathsome creatures who can do no good, but that there is no privileged no-go area that sin does not crash, and no human act that is altogether uncompromised by self-interest. We think we call the shots. We don't. As grace goes all the way down in God, so sin goes all the way through in humans.

7. A Pauline anatomy of sin must also observe a crucial distinction between sin and sin*s*. Paul's fundamental harmatological category is not sins as moral failures but sin as an alien and enslaving power. Consequently Paul almost never speaks of the forgiveness of sins, or repentance; rather he speaks of sin's defeat and conquest by Jesus Christ—the sinless one. Indeed that is how we gauge just how radical and universal sin actually is: it takes the life, death, and resurrection of Christ to break it. Deducing the problem from the solution, Paul sees that without grace we would never know just how hopeless is the human condition.

---

4. Alistair McFadyen, *Bound to Sin: Abuse, Holocaust and the Christian Doctrine of Sin* (Cambridge: Cambridge University Press, 2000).

8. You know the phrase "ugly as sin"? Whenever I think of it I picture Duccio's "The Temptation of Christ on the Mountain" with its nightmarish figure of the devil. I also catch a whiff of Luther's shitty Satan. But how could the utterly repulsive be so totally tempting? Consider, then, the film *The Devil's Advocate* (1997), in which Al Pacino plays a Lucifer whose drop-dead attractiveness contributes as much as his corporate clout to his guile and persuasiveness. His text might come from the Rolling Stones song "Sympathy for the Devil" (inspired, incidentally, by another modern retelling of the Faust legend, Mikhail Bulgakov's *The Master and Margarita*): "Please allow me to introduce myself, I'm a man of wealth and taste." Sin is no Ugly Betty.

9. On the other hand, the devil is a liar. He makes sin seem so exciting, both as lust and lure to power. "Work on their horror of the Same Old Thing," C. S. Lewis' Screwtape advises his nephew Wormwood.[5] In fact, sin itself always turns out to be unoriginal, recycled, predictable, dead boring—the Same Old Thing. But Satan is so streetwise that, like gullible teenagers or old folk with bad memories, we are always falling for his provocative promises. Thus P. T. Barnum could have been speaking of original sin when he said, "There's a sucker born every minute." By the way, one of the best antidotes to temptation is a sense of humor. Like all tyrants, the devil insists on being taken seriously, so take the mickey and remove the sting.

10. Finally, a crucial pastoral point, based on an acute theological insight of Karl Barth, which Deborah van Deusen Hunsinger puts powerfully and succinctly: "The paradox of the knowledge of human sin is that human beings can ultimately know themselves as sinners only in the light of forgiveness. Known sin as such ... is always finally forgiven sin. We cannot fully

---

5. C. S. Lewis, *The Screwtape Letters* (Glasgow: Collins, 1987 [first published in 1942]), p. 126.

perceive ourselves as sinners ... apart from Jesus Christ."[6] Which is why repentance, rightly understood, cannot possibly mire one in guilt, shame, and depression; rather, as a homecoming, it is ultimately an act of sheer joy.

6. Deborah van Deusen Hunsinger, *Theology and Pastoral Counselling: A New Interdisciplinary Approach* (Grand Rapids, Michigan: William B. Eerdmans, 1995), p. 195.

Do I love God? How can I know?

Do I love God? How can I know?
　By following the rules?
No, rules are guides that can't divide
　the faithful from the fool.

Do I love God? How can I know?
　By keeping to the creeds?
No, right belief brings no relief
　from doubts that grow like weeds.

Do I love God? How can I know?
　By looking deep within?
No, introspection's always marred
　by self-deceit and sin.

Do I love God? How can I know?
　I can't, but I can trust
the God whose grace I can't escape,
　whose judgement's more than just.

Do I love God? How can I know?
　I can't — but here's the key:
I love God only as I love
　the ones who don't love me.

Ten Propositions on Self-Love

1. There is a lot of horse manure talked about "self-love." Allow me to wield a pitchfork and begin a cleanout of this particular Augean stable, the whiff of which has become unbearable in our shamelessly therapeutic culture. It is, of course, no coincidence that the triumph of global capitalism, achieved on the whole by osmosis rather than bloodshed, has been accompanied by the saturation of the therapeutic in everyday life: international policing is such a clumsy means of social control compared to self-inflicted pleasure. The slogan of the sixties rebranded for the noughties: "Make love to your self, not war."

2. It is often said that self-love is commanded in the Bible itself: "Love your neighbor as yourself." Such a reading of this text suggests either wishful thinking or exegesis gone on holiday. Luther and Calvin read more accurately and insightfully: they saw that neighbor-love begins only where self-love ends, and vice-versa. As Robert Jenson observes: "Though it is sometimes supposed that Scripture's famous mandate makes self-love a standard which our love for the other is to emulate, the relation in Scripture works the other way; Scripture contains no mention of self-love except as a foil for love of the other. The object of love is always other than the love."[1]

3. How, in fact, do we love ourselves? With a passion — the passion of distorted desire — which is to say with utter self-absorption. How are we to love others? With precisely that as-myself absorption — but directed entirely to the other-than-myself. The paradigms are the Trinity and the cross. Self-love looks inwards; in contrast, observe the gazes, the looks of love of Father, Son, and Holy Spirit, in Rublev's famous icon. Self-

---

1. Robert Jenson, *On Thinking the Human: Resolutions of Difficult Notions* (Grand Rapids, Michigan: William B. Eerdmans, 2003), p. 55.

love is full of itself; in contrast, other-love is empty of self. It is kenotic (cf. Philippians 2:1–11).

4. Am I saying that we should hate ourselves? Heaven forbid! Self-hatred simply plays Tweedledum to self-love's Tweedledee: both are equally forms of self-centeredness, of Luther's *homo incurvatus in se*. So too, by the way, is "sincerity," which is usually but self-deceit masquerading as transparency, the sign of a person taken in by his own act (as in hand-on-heart politicians). "Complete self-confidence," wrote Chesterton, "is not merely a sin; complete self-confidence is a weakness."[2] People who are fond of quoting Shakespeare's words, "To thine own self be true," should recall that it is the sententious buffoon Polonius who speaks them. We must be delivered from self altogether, such that "It is no longer I who live, but it is Christ who lives in me" (Galatians 2:20).

5. What about the nostrum "Love the sinner but hate the sin"? It sounds so intuitively right as to be unquestionable. But is the person so easily separable from the work? Is sin merely accidental? Is it not dispositional, even ontological? An anthropological can of worms opens! Suffice it to say for this discussion that even if it is a distinction that can be drawn in principle, "loving the sinner but hating the sin," as a populist ethic, is usually more honored in the breach than the observance, amounting to the sheerest humbug. Look at the way the rhetoric of evil is deployed to deny the human rights of terrorists or the dignity of paedophiles. Or simply ask a gay Christian if he feels loved by the church that regards him as a sinner.

6. But to return to the main thread: "self-esteem" is the particularly modernist version of self-love (not postmodernist: in postmodernism there *is* no self to love or esteem!). It goes with the demise of the discourse of sin and guilt, and the ascendancy of

---

2. G. K. Chesterton, *Orthodoxy* (London: Hodder & Stoughton, 1996 [first published in 1908]), p. 9.

the culture of narcissism (and victimhood): the nonsense of "I'm okay, you're okay." Here we lose all contact with reality, because I'm *not* okay, I suck—and you do too. Well, don't you? (If you don't think you do, I refer you to Jeremiah 17:9.) Alcoholics Anonymous is closer to the truth: "I'm not okay, and you're not okay, but that's okay."

7. But *why* is that okay? Because—and only because—Christ died for our unokayness are we okay, okay with *God* and therefore *really* okay—which is a rather vulgar restatement of the Reformation doctrine of the justification of the sinner. Ours is an "alien" okayness, an okayness *extra nos*, but this is not a fiction, and indeed it is precisely on the basis of the divine imprimatur that we are freed *from* self-love *for* other-love (which is why AA's "but that's okay" requires a supplement: to Luther's justification of the sinner, add Calvin's justification of the righteous, or regeneration). In more felicitous non-religious language, Paul Tillich rephrased the justification of the sinner as the "acceptance of the unacceptable." Given—but only given—the *sola gratia*, perhaps "self-acceptance" is the word we are looking for. But even that is not the end of the matter ...

8. I suggest that there are huge implications here for so-called Christian spirituality. I say "so-called" because in fact much of what now passes for Christian spirituality is simply cod psychology with a halo. Who, for example, needs the desert fathers when you've got James Fowler's "Stages of Faith" (faith without an object), or the Myers-Briggs Type Indicator (personality without character—or spirit)? And "inner healing" remains a big buzzword on the spirituality circuit. The presumption would seem to be that "God loves only those who love themselves" (cf. managerialism's "God helps only those who help themselves"), with its corollary that only as we love ourselves can we love others.

9. But this is a formula for the crassest form of works-righteousness, indeed practical atheism (cf. managerialism's relentless Pelagianism), as well as a recipe for spiritual pride—or de-

spair. Were the Reformers not right that God's love for us is a
free gift that has nothing whatsoever to do with self-feeling or
self-construction? Can we not trust that God's unconditional
grace is sufficient to all our needs? Is not that the only way we
can honestly acknowledge, without self-loathing, the old Adam,
that compulsive recidivist and persistent squatter, even as we
learn to live the liberation we already have, hidden in Christ?
And have not the great saints themselves taught us that the
Holy Spirit both drives us to and guides us through our experiences of alienation and woundedness, precisely to deepen
our trust in God and to enlarge the range of our compassion?

10. Writing of the nineteenth-century Abbé Marie-Joseph Huvelin,
Rowan Williams observes that he "was not what many would
call a whole man," that he "lived with a sense of his own worth-
lessness almost unrelieved by the hope and assurance he trans-
mitted to so many others." And the question Williams poses is
this: "can we, with our rhetoric of the identity of holiness and
wholeness, begin to cope with the 'sanctity' of a man whose
mental and emotional balance was so limited? A man less than
perfectly sane. We do not here have to do simply with the question of the *holy fool*, but the question—harder for our day—
of the holy neurotic."[3] A question we'd better answer before we
sell a great theological heritage and spiritual tradition for a
mess of Jungianism.

3. Rowan Williams, "The Abbé Huvelin: A University Sermon for All
Saints Day", in *Open to Judgement: Sermons and Addresses* (London: Darton, Longman and Todd, 1994), p. 208.

Lord, we thank you for tradition

Lord, we thank you for tradition,
    for the Fathers and the Creeds,
for Reformers' erudition,
    speaking to the church's needs.

And we thank you for their power
    to transcend a single time,
pressing on the present hour
    with still fruitful paradigms.

But, Lord, save us from supposing
    that our calling's to repeat
what the church once said, so closing
    minds to truths yet incomplete.

Teach us, Lord, the past's potential
    for creation, not control,
lest we, seeking what's essential,
    take the partial for the whole.

When we see your glory blazing,
    our best thoughts will seem like straw;
how can human words and phrasing
    capture God who's always more?

Ten Propositions on Heresy

1. Heresy comes from the Greek *hairesis* (literally "choice" or "thing chosen") and denotes an "opinion" or a "school of thought." In I Corinthians 11:19 the RSB translates *haireseis* as "divisions," the NRSV as "factions"; and while Paul suggests that "there have to be (*dei*) factions among you," as a way of separating the wheat from the chaff, nevertheless, as the context confirms, he deploys the word in a negative sense. See also the list of vices ("works of the flesh") in Galatians 5:20: "factions" (NRSV), "party intrigues" (REB).

2. Of course what constitutes heresy is not pre-packaged; there is no timeless, pure dogma, discovered, *simpliciter*, like a diamond already cut. On the other hand, a purely constructivist account of orthodoxy is inadequate, as if it were costume jewelry. There is a real sense in which dogma gives expression to what has been *given* to the church from the beginning, what the church already knows before it recognizes it, yet comes to recognize only through relentless arguments about it, arguments issuing in fine and fragile articulations that say neither too little nor too much, and sometimes say it in negatives (cf. the apophaticism of the Chalcedonian Definition). "Orthodoxy," Auden always insisted, "is reticence."

3. The early cuts, set in the creeds, were made in the context of ferocious Christological controversies. In dispute was the very identity of God, the God who creates and redeems us, to whom the church witnesses — and prays. *Lex orandi, lex credendi*. The context was liturgical: doctrine is doxological. The arguments were not "academic," what was at stake was "personal": the experience of salvation in Christ, and the transmission, through careful conversation, of the parameters within which the experience may be realized. Augustine called sound doctrine the hedge that protects the field where the Christian encounters God. I would add only that a hedge is made of shrubs, not bricks and barbed wire.

4. Another image: if orthodoxy is the bull's eye, heresy is, as Rowan Williams puts it, the "near-misses"—which actually help guide the church towards the target (cf. Schleiermacher's reference to his own teaching on God as "inspired heterodoxy"). The early heretics were generally neither knaves nor fools but pious and passionate men, zealous for God, morally serious, scrupulously scriptural. They were very clever, but conventional, fetchers and carriers for the zeitgeist. Heretics like a "wrap," and heresies are fastidiously neat and tidy, the product of minds stuck inside the box of common sense. "Consistency," said Oscar Wilde, "is the last refuge of the unimaginative." Unsurprisingly, then, heresy is aesthetically unattractive, even ugly.

5. I think it was Alfred North Whitehead who said that there are no such things as whole truths, there are only half-truths, and treating half-truths like whole truths plays the devil. Whitehead might have been talking about heresy. Heretics are one-eyed, they lack the "vision thing": failing to see the bigger picture, they take the part for the whole. That is why heresy is inevitably rather boring. Heretics have no sense of adventure; they go only so far, they won't go "all the way." You could say they are theological prudes, often wearing philosophical chastity belts, who resist being ravished by revelation.

6. Marcion was a literalist who couldn't get his head around the apparent contradictions between Old and New Testaments, and so he hacked the Bible in two. Arius was monomaniacally monotheist and uncompromisingly conservative and resistant to conceptual innovation; his "notion of unity is devoid of the richness—and the mystery—of God's unity. It is devoid of the unity of love."[1] Eutyches was "a confused and unskilled thinker ... blindly rushing forward to defend the unity of Christ against all attempts to divide Him";[2] while Nestorius, if not

---

1. Arthur C. McGill, *Suffering: A Test of Theological Method* (Philadelphia: The Westminster Press, 1982), p. 77.

2. J. N. D. Kelly, *Early Christian Doctrines* (London: Adam & Charles Black, 1977 [first published in 1958]), p. 333.

perhaps a Nestorian, launched such a "maladroit, crudely expressed exposition of the implications of the Antiochene position"[3] on the two natures of Christ that he was never able to explain coherently what constitutes his center.

7. And then there are those perennial pests, Pelagianism and Donatism (technically a "schism," an error of love rather than faith). A fair-minded comparison of Augustine's exegesis with Pelagius' interpretation of Psalm 14, and Donatus' interpretation of the parable of the Wheat and the Tares, is initially embarrassing.[4] But when the bishop of Hippo raises the bar, deconstructing the human soul and insisting that God is always greater than we think, the two heresiarchs—the one monkish and severe, the other hawkish and charismatic, both perfectionists—are out of their depths. They are noble figures, and theirs are heroic theologies, but—Augustine's legacy—God calls us to be saints, not heroes, people aware of their brokenness and need of healing, stray lambs longing for the flock's welcome and warmth, and for a shepherd to lead them home.

8. "Remember," wrote Chesterton, "that the church went in specifically for dangerous ideas; she was a lion tamer.... This is the thrilling romance of Orthodoxy. People have fallen into the foolish habit of speaking of orthodoxy as something heavy, humdrum, and safe. There never was anything so perilous or so exciting as orthodoxy. It was sanity: and to be sane is more dramatic than to be mad."[5] And the mark of the mad: "this combination between a logical completeness and a spiritual contraction."[6] And so: "Whenever we feel that there is something

---

3. Ibid., p. 310.

4. I owe these examples to Nicholas Adams and Ben Quash in Ben Quash and Michael Ward (eds.), *Heresies and How to Avoid Them* (London: SPCK, 2007), pp. 97–98 and pp. 87–88.

5. G. K. Chesterton, *Orthodoxy* (London: Hodder & Stoughton, 1996 [first published in 1908]), pp. 145–46.

6. Ibid., p. 18.

odd in Christian theology, we shall generally find that there is something odd in the truth."[7] Heresy is uncomfortable with the oddness of God.

9. "The truth of dogmas does not depend on the fact that the church maintains them. But is this really so? This is an abiding question, and dogmatics must always leave it open!"[8] Tradition should get the benefit of the doubt, but might some of it be but "agedness of error" (Milton)? An ancient dogma, now widely contested, is the divine impassibility. With Moltmann, Jüngel declares that the cross has abrogated the principles of divine immutability and *apatheia*. Process and liberation theologians join the troops, while Thomas Weinandy, John Milbank, and David Bentley Hart mount rearguard actions. Were the Theopaschites (if not the Patripassianists) right after all? In any case, claims to infallibility — a kind of tradition fundamentalism — bring orthodoxy into disrepute, and church history is littered with enough ill-conceived defenses of orthodoxy to warrant theological vigilance and modesty. Moreover (in Wittgenstein's image drawn from chess), while doubt plays black to trust, the acute post-enlightenment awareness of the historical and social location of ideas, and the undeniable insights of *Tendenzkritik* regarding the power-interests that texts serve and legitimate, entail a loss of dogmatic innocence that must give suspicion its due. When Christians boast of their orthodoxy, check your pockets. And, of course, orthodoxy itself tells us that no one is saved by his orthodoxy.

10. Finally, what do you do with heretics? Burn 'em? Or at least track them down and corner them? If you've got a magisterium, you can fire the Küngs and the Currans. If you're a powerful and aggressive church leader, you can threaten to take your ball

---

7. Ibid., p. 117.

8. Gerhard Sauter, *Gateways to Dogmatics* (Grand Rapids, Michigan: William B. Eerdmans, 2003), p. 26.

and go home while at the same time invading other pitches (or is it Bishop Akinola who is the [Donatist] heretic?). Karl Barth warned against witch-hunts against Bultmann, and the author of the Barmen Declaration called the contemporary "confessional movement" tawdry and pharisaical. On the other hand, I'm sure Barth would have approved of declaring apartheid a heresy. Finally, however, Stanley Hauerwas is right: "That one of the tests of orthodoxy is beauty means orthodoxy betrays itself if it is used as a hammer to beat into submission those we think heterodox."[9] And, of course, unless orthodoxy itself issues in orthopraxis — because truth is not so much thought as done (John 7:17) — well, hypocrisy isn't heresy, but it ain't pretty. The telos of orthodoxy is not conformity but faith-working-through-love in joyful obedience.

---

9. Stanley Hauerwas, in Ben Quash and Michael Ward (eds.), *Heresies and How to Avoid Them*, p. x.

What happens after death?

What happens after death?
  Will humans live again?
Is nothingness the destiny
  that marks our final end?

Does heaven lie above?
  Is hell a pit of fire?
Do all get just what they deserve
  or what their hearts desire?

What happens after death?
  Of course we live again!
From nothingness God spoke his word
  of life—and life's our end.

Yes, heaven is a place,
  but not a place above,
it's found in God's geography,
  located in his love.

And, yes, there is a hell,
  a state of black despair,
but Christ assumes what we deserve,
  so not a soul is there.

Our hope is Christ alone,
  divine humanity,
who lived and died and lives again
  for all eternity.

Ten Propositions on Hell

1. What is hell? Hell cannot be known in and of itself. As a negative to a positive, hell can be known only as the antithesis of heaven. Heaven is life with God, hell is the absence of God.

   Hell is neither here nor there,
   Hell is not anywhere,
   Hell is hard to bear.
   (W. H. Auden, "Hell")

2. Because God is love, hell is lovelessness. At its center, hell is not hot, hell (as Dante saw) is cold—*ice*-cold. The expression "When hells freezes over"—it should be, "When hell melts." Or if, with most Christian tradition, hell be aflame, "Yet from those flames/No light, but rather darkness visible" (Milton, *Paradise Lost*, I/62–63).

3. What is the opposite of love? Not hatred. Hatred is the smoke above the inferno of fear. That is why St. John says, "Perfect love casts out fear" (I John 4:18)—and throws it into hell. Hell is the war *of* terror. Some, however, hold that indifference is the opposite of love. In which case hell is absolute boredom. In Beckett's *Waiting for Godot*, Estragon says: "Nothing happens, nobody comes, nobody goes, it's awful!"

4. And hell is despair, *utter* despair. Dante again: "Abandon hope, all you who enter here." Jesus said that "the gate is wide and the road is easy that leads to destruction" (Matthew 7:13). He might have added that there are also many entrances—but no exits. Hell is viciously circular.

5. The one who reigns in hell is an absolute monarch, ruling with coercive, violent, destructive power (*potestas absoluta*). "The devil took him to a very high mountain and showed him all the kingdoms of the world and their splendor; and he said to him, 'All these things I will give you ...'" (Matthew 4:8–9).

6. Heaven is communion, hell is isolation. Sartre was wrong: hell is not other people, hell is me, myself, and I. Milton's Satan: "Which way I fly is Hell; myself am Hell" (IV/75). Hell is full of rats gnawing their own tails.

7. I can speak properly of hell only if I speak in the first person singular, as one who knows he is capable of pouring Zyklon B into a chamber full of children. The demonic I see in others is always a reflection of my own lost soul. Of one thing we can be sure about anyone who knows the population of hell: he himself will be in the census.

8. Hell is not about what God does, hell is about what we do, about the horrendous evils we commit, the holocausts we start and stoke. We deceive ourselves, indeed we lie—we prove ourselves offspring of Satan, who is "the father of lies" (John 8:44)— if we deny the reality of hell. And we betray the victims of the anti-world in which we live.

9. Yet hell is not a datum of faith in the creeds. "I believe in the resurrection of the body, and the life everlasting" (The Apostles' Creed). "We look for the resurrection of the dead, and the life of the world to come" (The Nicene Creed). We do not believe *in* hell.

10. Therefore while hell is real, we may pray and hope that hell will finally be empty—and that if it is not empty I will be on my own. Universalism? "This much is certain, that we have no theological right to set any sort of limits to the loving-kindness of God which has appeared in Jesus Christ. Our theological duty is to see and understand it as being still greater than we had seen it before."[1] Thus the church will not *preach* hell —"the gospel at gun-point"[2]—it will preach grace, grace, and

---

1. Karl Barth, *The Humanity of God* (Great Britain: Collins, 1961), p. 60.

2. Karl Barth, cited in Eberhard Busch, *Karl Barth* (London: SCM Press, 1976), p. 446.

grace again, triumphant in the cross (Christ experiencing hell) and the resurrection (Christ harrowing hell).

The steadfast love of the Lord never ceases,
his mercies never come to an end.
(Lamentations 3:22)

God whose presence is an absence

God whose presence is an absence,
   never like an object "there",
speak to me in sounds of silence,
   in the voiceless void of prayer.

God whose truth's beyond all showing,
   not like one and one are two,
teach us truth's not known by knowing,
   truth is something that we do.

God whose being is an ocean,
   sea of love yet unexplored,
keep my flailing faith in motion
   as I paddle by the shore.

God who keeps a proper distance,
   God who runs ahead at pace,
leave us signs of your existence,
   footprints we may track and trace.

When in heaven we behold you,
   with the angels, face to face,
we will see that all we've been through
   was the trailer of your grace.

Ten Propositions on
Richard Dawkins and the New Atheists

1. Richard Dawkins and the New Atheists do not like Christians. They like Muslims even less. We are like people who believe in leprechauns, only worse, because people who believe in leprechauns, while ignoramuses, are not warmongers and terrorists (unless they also happen to be Irish Catholics or Presbyterians). So the New Atheists are our enemies. But remember, Jesus said that we should love our enemies, forgive them, and pray for them. That will really get on their nerves.

2. But Dawkins is not just angry with Christians, with particular dismay at scientists who are Christians (who, of course, are huge flies in his ointment — at the word "Polkinghorne" he grinds his teeth). Dawkins also gets angry with fellow scientists on scientific matters. One of his most bitter and public altercations was with the late Stephen Jay Gould, the famous Harvard palaeontologist. The religious affairs correspondent Andrew Brown wrote a book documenting this *rabies biologorum*: it's called *The Darwin Wars*. So you've got to be fair to Dawkins, he is evenly balanced: he has a chip on both shoulders.

3. I should point out that the word "wars" in *The Darwin Wars* is (I think) a metaphor. Dawkins himself has a knack for the memorable metaphor. His great book *The Selfish Gene* is a case in point. People can be literally selfish, but not genes. Indeed Dawkins does not even think that there are genes for selfishness. Okay, he wrote: "The gene is the basic unit of selfishness."[1] But he didn't really mean it. Not literally. The author of Genesis said that the universe was created in six days. But who would take that literally except some crazy fundamentalists? Oops — and Dawkins.

---

1. Richard Dawkins, *The Selfish Gene* (Oxford: Oxford University Press, 2006 [first published in 1976]), p. 36.

4. In *The God Delusion* Dawkins suggests (no, he states—Dawkins doesn't do "suggests") that "the Christian focus is overwhelmingly on sin sin sin sin sin sin sin." No commas, unrelenting. And count them: that's sin x 7. Perhaps this is a clever allusion to Matthew 18:21. After all, even the devil quotes scripture. The self-proclaimed Devil's Chaplain continues: "What a nasty little preoccupation to have dominating your life."[2] Yes, we Christians think of little else. But here's a thought. All those wars like the one in Iraq that Christopher Hitchens is so keen on, or the practice of torture that Sam Harris says is necessary —that couldn't have anything to do with our "focus," could it?

5. Their teaching on sin shows the New Atheists to be true children of the Enlightenment—that and their belief in religionless "progress." Now Dawkins' case against faith is that it is "belief without evidence." (For the sake of argument, never mind that this definition itself is belief *against* the evidence.) So on his own terms we may be permitted to ask Dawkins, "Where is the evidence for this progress?" Forgive me, dear reader, for wearying you with the obvious: the names of such progressive statesmen and harbingers of world peace as the atheists Joseph Stalin, Mao Tse-Tung, and Pol Pot. Oh, and isn't there the little matter that teleology has no place in evolutionary theory? Progress? My money is on the leprechauns.

6. "Imagine someone holding forth on biology whose only knowledge of the subject is the *Book of British Birds,* and you have a rough idea of what it feels like to read Richard Dawkins on theology."[3] After this now famous first-line knockdown punch by Terry Eagleton it would be unsportsmanlike to bully the bully. Dawkins does not enter the ring with the intellectual heavyweights of the Christian tradition, though he occasionally

2. Richard Dawkins, *The God Delusion* (London: Bantam Press, 2006), p. 252.

3. Terry Eagleton, "Lunging, Flailing, Mispunching", *London Review of Books*, 19 October, 2006.

throws a bottle at them from the seats. Is he ignorant, hubristic, or just plain chicken? Whatever. The irony is that Dawkins thereby again betrays the very Enlightenment he represents, "everything that the Western intellectual tradition stands for, with its privileging of informed scholarship based on the study of texts."[4]

7. If Dawkins is the "bad cop" of the New Atheists, the *Guardian* journalist Polly Toynbee is probably the "good cop," while Christopher Hitchens is undoubtedly the "corrupt cop." I saw him on the British TV programme *Question Time*, contemptuously holding court like Jabba the Hutt. And I sat for half-an-hour at Waterstone's bookshop dipping into the over-priced *God Is Not Great* as if it were dishwater, a highly flattering simile. Hitchens' penetrating scholarly appraisals include descriptions of Augustine the "ignoramus,"[5] Aquinas the "stupid,"[6] and Calvin the "sadist";[7] while Niemöller and Bonhoeffer's resistance to the Nazis was motivated by a"nebulous humanism,"[8] and Martin Luther King's faith was Christian only in a "nominal sense."[9] Enough said. It is all rather embarrassing.

8. There are two reactions to this sort of illiteracy that must be avoided. The first is the response of the right, which, when not hysterical, simply confirms the unquestioned assumption of the New Atheists that God is a huge and powerful supernatural being whose ways with the world are, in principle, open to empirical discovery and verification. This is the God of In-

---

4. As Tina Beattie records a comment Keith Ward made to her, sadly, in *The New Atheists: The Twilight of Reason and the War on Religion* (London: Darton, Longman and Todd, 2007), p. 16.

5. Christopher Hitchens, *God Is Not Great: The Case against Religion* (London: Atlantic Books, 2007), p. 64).

6. Ibid., p. 64.

7. Ibid., p. 233.

8. Ibid., p. 7.

9. Ibid., p. 176.

telligent Design. If ID is science, it is either bad science or dead science. "Bring it on!" cries Professor Dawkins, gleefully rubbing his hands together. But even if it were good science (and even if it weren't driven by a political agenda), it would be dreadful, indeed suicidal theology, for the god of ID is but a version of the "god of the gaps," a god deployed as an explanation of natural phenomena, a hostage to scientific fortune, in short, an idol. The operation of ID can be successful only at the cost of the patient.

9. The second response is the response of the left, the liberals. On this Enlightenment view, science is given its due in the realm of "facts," while religion is cordoned off from the New Atheists in the realm of "values." There is a superficial attractiveness to this division of territory—Stephen Jay Gould called it "NOMA," or Non-Overlapping Magisteria, separate but equal—but in the end it amounts to theological appeasement. For the realm of "facts" includes not only the empirical, natural world but also the embodied, public, political world, while religion becomes the sphere of the "spiritual," the interior, and the private. The church cannot accept this partition for Leviathan, the nation state, is a violent and voracious beast. Nor, however, is the church called to become the state: theocracies are inevitably gross distortions of power, whether the flag bears a cross or a crescent. Rather the church is called to be a distinctive polis forming citizens for the kingdom of God and sending them into the kingdoms of the world as truth-tellers and peacemakers.

10. The New Atheists don't only have a dashing if reckless officer leading an army of grunts, they also have their aesthetes, a brilliant novelist in Ian McEwan, a master fantasist in Philip Pullman. Are they dangerous? Of course! Yet if the Russian expressionist painter Alexei Jawlensky was right that "all art is nostalgia for God," there is nothing to fear and something to gain from them, their didacticism notwithstanding. Unlike atheist writers such as Camus or Beckett who have been to the

altar but cannot kneel, McEwan and Pullman are unacquainted with the God of Jesus. Nevertheless, McEwan, in novels like *Enduring Love, Atonement,* and *Saturday* (titles freighted with theological irony), so elegantly probes the human shadows, and Pullman, in the *His Dark Materials* trilogy (the title drawn from *Paradise Lost*), so imaginatively narrates the themes of innocence and experience and exposes the corruptions of false religion, that we feel at least that we have been in the outer courts of the temple. It is certainly better to read this literature and be disturbed by it than not to read it at all.

Serious Fun

God who creates and then colors the earth

God who creates and then colors the earth,
paints it with beautiful features—
oceans and islands, and forests and beasts—
preparing for reasoning creatures.

> *Sinful or pure, doubtful or sure,*
> *God comes to those who are ready or not;*
> *woman or male, healthy or frail,*
> *God wants us all to be part of the plot.*

God who calls Adam and Noah and Abe,
Moses and monarchs and seers,
fashions a people he claims for his own—
how odd!—in the land of Judea.

God who sends angels to Mary and Joe,
earthing the dream of Isaiah,
guides surprised shepherds and wise men to go
and witness the birth of Messiah.

God who empowers the Christ in his work,
scribes and disciples amazing,
sends his own Son to his suffering and death,
but saves the whole world by his raising.

God who continues his mission through saints—
folk overwhelmed by his glory;
still he is here after zillions of years
and writing us into his story.

Ten Propositions on Faith and Laughter

1. Let's face it: the Bible is not exactly a barrel of laughs. In the Old Testament the Lord laughs a few times in the Psalms—at the nations' rulers in Psalm 2:4, at the wicked and godless in Psalms 37:13 and 59:8—but it is a disdainful, derisive laughter. As for human laughter, the preacher in Ecclesiastes 2:2 calls it "foolish" (GNB), "mad" (NRSV), even if it does have its "time" (cf. 3:4); while Job's so-called comforters, Eliphaz and Bildad, console their friend with the promise of laughter if he repents (5:22, 8:21)—but we know what God thinks of them (42:7).

2. Is Sarah an exception? She laughs when God promises her a child in her dotage, but beneath her breath (Genesis 18:12). But the Lord hears her giggling—"Yeah, right!" she is thinking—and he is not amused at her doubt, so in fear she denies that she laughed (18:15a). "Oh yes you did!" the Lord replies (18:15b). We should remember that Abraham laughed too when told that Sarah would bear him a child (17:17), but evidently our (sexist?) Lord was more indulgent with the old man than with his old lady. One thing is for sure: juxtapose the two scenes and you have the stuff of situation comedy!

3. And then there is the name "Isaac"—"the one who will laugh". Does giving the child of promise such a sobriquet suggest that God has a sense of humor after all? And perhaps we should not overlook the additional syllables that God adds to the names Abram and Sarai: they become AbrAHam and SarAH—"an onomatopoeic 'Ha-Ha.'"[1]

4. There are three explicit references to laughter in the New Testament. In James 4:9 the complacent laughter-become-mourning of repentance; in Matthew 9:24 (par. Mark 5:40, Luke 8:53) the dismissive laughter of the crowd at a funeral that Jesus

---

1. Simon Critchley, *On Humour* (London: Routledge, 2002), p. 42.

crashes; and in Luke 6:25 the smug laughter of the powerful
—and in Luke 6:21 the eschatological laughter of the powerless. The eschatological laughter is promising, even proleptic.
For if the verbal abuse of Jesus' enemies at the foot of the cross
surely included cruel and mocking laughter, may we not suggest an Easter laughter—*risus paschalis*—that rings out with
resurrection joy?

5. Did Jesus laugh? The fictional dispute in Umberto Eco's novel
The Name of the Rose, set in the Middle Ages, "is more than
fiction. It reflects a line of tradition which really existed, from
John Chrysostom through Augustine to Bernard of Clairvaux
and Hugo of St. Victor, of the Christian denunciation of laughter."[2] Nor is such a "theology of tears" limited to the world-
denying, death-obsessed medieval zeitgeist. John Wesley once
disciplined a preacher on the charges (in ascending order?) of
heresy, adultery—and the man's proneness to "break a jest,
and laugh at it heartily." Here, from Samuel Beckett's *Molloy*,
Moran debates the issue with Father Ambrose, who sides with
Eco's character Jorge (a Dominican—who is blind):

"What a joy it is to laugh, from time to time, he said. Is it not?
I said. It is peculiar to man, he said. So I have noticed, I said.
A brief silence ensued [...] Animals never laugh, he said. It
takes us to find that funny, I said. What? he said. It takes us to
find that funny, I said loudly. He mused. Christ never laughed
either, he said, so far as we know. He looked at me. Can you
wonder? I said."[3]

6. You laughed, right? Christ, I reckon, would have cracked up too.
Did he not have a Beckett-like sense of the absurd (gnats and
camels, logs and splinters), the ironic (calling Simon a *Petros*
[Rock], telling fishermen where to fish), and even the coarse

---

2. Karl-Josef Kuschel, *Laughter: A Theological Reflection* (London: SCM
Press, 1994), p. 43.

3. Samuel Beckett, *Molloy*, (London: Calder and Boyars, 1959), p. 109.

(suggesting that one go naked in court [Matthew 5:40], insinuating that the Pharisees are full of crap [Mark 7:15]). And is anyone going to tell me that a man who likes to party, with a reputation to go with it, doesn't like a laugh? So with many a Renaissance Humanist, Eco's William of Baskerville (a Franciscan, one of God's "merry men"—who can see because he wears spectacles) was surely right: of course Jesus laughed! A limerick comes to me:

> In the O.T. our God the Most High
> in his folk put *timor Domini*,
> but in Jesus his Son
> he earthed Word-play and pun:
> like a mushroom, he was a fun-guy.

7. The only serious theological question is not "Did Jesus laugh?" but "Did Jesus laugh in his divinity as well as his humanity?" As with suffering, the doctrine of the divine impassibility would suggest not. If, however, revisionists like Moltmann and Jüngel are right, then if God can suffer, surely God can also laugh. The resurrection event is crucial, as it identifies—perhaps even constitutes—the very being of God. In any case, the grammar of faith allows, and (I submit) the substance of faith demands the statement: "God laughs"—and not only with scorn for his enemies but, above all, with joy for his friends.

8. Ergo, an Easter people cannot act like lemon-suckers. Chesterton said that "Angels can fly because they take themselves lightly," and no less an authority than the Angelic Doctor himself "leaves the Christian with a wide field for his fun. He does so on the authority of the Philosopher"—revelation and reason in perfect harmony—"who, we are reminded, 'posits the virtue of eutrapelia, which in Latin we call *jucunditas,* enjoyment.' His conclusion rejoices smiling Christians."[4] Alas, St. Thomas set limits to Christian frivolity: no dirty jokes! Calvin agreed—

4. M. A. Screech, *Laughter at the Foot of the Cross* (London: Penguin, 1997), p. 136.

but not scatologically-minded Luther. And Erasmus, while keen on wit, disapproved of tickling—which, in my view, comes close to advocating child abuse.

9. There is a *political* dimension to laughter, namely laughter as protest and resistance, disarming tyrant or terrorist with ecstatic power. "Laugh and fear not, creatures," declares C. S. Lewis' famous lion Aslan, "for jokes as well as justice come in with speech." Humor has been particularly important in sustaining the children of Moses in the wilderness of oppression, not least in the face of Christian anti-Semitism. Hence the extensive corpus of Jewish jokes about Christians, doleful and yearning, yet also acerbic. Like this one:

The priest says to the rabbi: "There are three things I can't stand about you Jews: you wander about the synagogue, you pray noisily, and your funerals are chaotic." The rabbi replies: "We wander about the synagogue because we feel at home there. We pray noisily because Yahweh is old and hard of hearing. And as for funerals, we too prefer the Christian ones."

And there is the Jewish character, figure of fun, known as the *schlemihl*: a rather weak, inept, and vulnerable guy who takes on the chin whatever goys throw at him, who gets knocked down again and again, but who always gets up, dusts himself off, and gets on with life without a grumble. There is a Christian version of the *schlemihl*: his name is Charlie Brown. In the *schlemihl* laughter is not only polemical critique, it is also therapeutic self-critique lest the oppressed becomes the oppressor.

10. Finally, the *liturgical* dimension of laughter: Is there a place for laughter in worship? One thing laughter and prayer have in common: they are both a waste of time (and therefore, by the way, profoundly anti-capitalist). However Reinhold Niebuhr asserted that there is no laughter in the Holy of Holies. So it's okay to crack a joke in the pulpit, perhaps, but not at the altar? But who has not laughed during the organized chaos that can be the passing of the peace? And if there are children at the

table, well, as Art Linkletter famously put it on his popular American TV show, "Kids say the darndest things!" And although the eucharist as anamnesis of the meal "on the night he was betrayed" is certainly a solemn moment, does not the eu-*charist* as anticipation of the Messiah's wedding feast invite making merry? Donald MacKinnon rightly pointed to the tragic elements in the Christian story, but his mentor Kierkegaard, depressive Dane that he was, judged it the most comical point of view in human history.

A personal anecdote. During my training for the ministry I was leading morning worship at Mansfield College, Oxford. Lesslie Newbigin was present, so I wanted to be word perfect. The Old Testament lesson, from I Samuel 14, was about Saul slaughtering the Philistines. I came to verse 15, which reads: "There was a panic in the camp." But this idiot read: "There was a *picnic* in the camp." As I prayed for the earth to open, all eyes turned to the great man. How would he respond? He laughed, of course!

St. Teresa prayed well: "Lord, preserve us from sullen saints."

Ten Reasons Why Baseball Is God's Game

The story is told of the aristocratic English cricket supporter who dies and appears at the Pearly Gates. St. Peter checks his list, but, alas, the old gentleman is not on it. "There must be some mistake," the man protests, "I have a permanent seat in the Lord's enclosure!"

Well, Lord's may be the home of cricket, but if cricket is heaven—and I write as an American expat who has lovingly lived in the UK for over thirty years—then heaven is as the cartoonist Larson depicts it: a bored bespectacled soul sitting on a cloud, thinking (in his thought balloon): "Wish I had a magazine." Cricket is indeed baseball on Valium, while baseball is "chess at ninety miles an hour" (Roger Kahn). Baseball is God's game. And here are just ten reasons why.

1. "The game of ball is glorious"—Walt Whitman. It begins in the spring—around Easter.

2. Baseball is about coming home. The whole point of the game is to finish where you begin—home plate, which is shaped like a house—and once you are home you are finally safe.

   "In my beginning is my end …
   Home is where one starts from …
   … In my end is my beginning."
   (T. S. Eliot, "East Coker")

3. Its rudiments come from another world, i.e. England (!); its beginnings are shrouded in myth and legend (Abner Doubleday, "Casey at the Bat," etc.); and its origins are pastoral, its destiny urban: it began in a garden and ends in the city. And the Original Sin: the banning of black players.

4. Its believers are nourished on Word and Sacrament: the umpire's shout, "Play ball!", and the pilgrim fare of Crackerjacks and soda, hotdogs and beer. And, amidst elaborate ritual, there is that numinous moment of stillness as the pitcher takes the sign, winds up, and delivers, and that most majestic of sounds—the crack of the bat (rubric: *All stand*).

5. It has its saints—e.g. Lou Gehrig (the Iron Horse) and Jackie Robinson (the first African-American player of the modern era)—and sinners—e.g. "Shoeless" Joe Jackson (who took a bribe) and Barry Bonds (who is alleged to have taken steroids). There is also the Great Satan: the New York Yankees. And while baseball players may make errors (sin), they receive no pennants (oops, penance!) from the long-suffering umpires, men in black suits (priests).

6. It has its cathedrals—ballparks, awesome, hallowed grounds, the immediate playing area the "diamond"—and its Temple in Jerusalem, the National Baseball Hall of Fame and Museum in Cooperstown, New York—replete with relics!

7. It had a Reformation with a splinter church, the American League—along with its ultimate descent into the heresy of the "designated hitter"! And yet the National and American League champions share in that great ecumenical act of worship known as the World Series.

8. It has its Suffering Servant: the Chicago Cubs, the "Cubbies," a team annually "led like a sheep to the slaughter" (Isaiah 53:7) (and crucial to the game is the play called the "sacrifice"). A history of the franchise might be called *A Hundred Years of Ineptitude*. But Cub fans divinely demonstrate a love that is unconditional, and conscientiously confirm that "faith is the assurance of things hoped for, the conviction of things not seen" (Hebrews 11:1).

9. Truly I tell you, whoever does not receive this game as a little child will never enter it (cf. Mark 10:15). Magically, baseball always brings out the child in you, and draws you back to your childhood, indeed makes your childhood present (*anamnesis*). And it is a tie that binds the generations, *communio sanctorum*.

10. Finally, baseball abounds in hope (cf. Romans 15:13). In every game, no matter what the score (as the legendary guru Yogi Berra famously put it): "It ain't over till it's over." At the end of every season, there is the irrepressible anticipation and cry

of "Next year!" Indeed baseball is ever full of redemptive eschatological promise: "If you build it, he will come" (*Field of
Dreams*). *Maranatha*!

Name Index